S0-DPQ-613

1.50
cxt

THE UNCUT NERVE OF MISSIONS

The Uncut Nerve of Missions

AN INQUIRY AND AN ANSWER

CLELAND BOYD McAFEE

*Board of Foreign Missions, Presbyterian
Church in the U. S. A.*

GENERAL THEOL. SEMINARY
LIBRARY
NEW YORK

NEW YORK
Fleming H. Revell Company
LONDON AND EDINBURGH

Copyright, MCMXXXII, by
FLEMING H. REVELL COMPANY

All rights reserved—no part of this book
may be reproduced in any form without
written permission from the publisher.

266T
M116
94567

GEN. THEO. SEMINARY
LIBRARY
NEW YORK

New York: 158 Fifth Avenue
London: 21 Paternoster Square

A PREFATORY WORD

THE figure of speech used in this small book should explain itself. It rests on the physical fact that when any member of the human body fails to move, the first investigation is of the nerve which runs to it. If that nerve is injured, impulses cannot be communicated to the organ.

The missionary activity of many churches and individual believers seems reduced, as is evidenced by reduced interest and support. The recession of gifts is not disturbing unless the reason back of it means the loss of real impulse. It is a common saying that this or that condition or opinion " cuts the nerve of missions," that is, checks or destroys the impulse toward missions. An effort is here made to examine the supposed changes which cut this nerve, to see if this result is warranted. Perhaps it comes from an original mistake of using and now losing impulses which were not the right ones. Or, it may come from misreading the new conditions. The inactivity of the missionary organ of the Church may result merely from neglect to use abiding impulses because of interest in nearer and more convenient demands. There may be as many good reasons for missionary zeal and as

5

mighty impulse toward it as ever, the changes accenting it rather than ending it.

The writer must not be supposed to be seeking to find out whether there are still good reasons for missions. He is not on the fence. He is squarely down on the missions side of it. But there are earnest people who have grave questions and who wonder what the future holds both of duty and of opportunity. An effort is here made to deal with these perfectly sincere questions.

C. B. McA.

156 Fifth Avenue,
New York.

CONTENTS

I

WHY SHOULD THE NERVE OF MISSIONS SEEM TO BE CUT?

THE missionary movement has always been sustained by a minority of Christian believers, and Christian believers in turn have always been a minority in society at large. Missionary work has therefore been the work of a minority of a minority.

However, it has now become so nearly world-wide that no world event can occur which does not at some point involve it. The so-called " mission lands " constitute more than half the area of the world with more than half the world's population. Any religion which attempts to extend its influence to all men must reckon at the very first with the necessity for changing a world minority into a majority. After a century of aggressive missionary work the most widespread faith in the world is the Christian religion. It cannot now be disregarded in newspapers or in public discussion.

In quiet times one can be neutral regarding missions. In such times as the world has been experiencing recently, this attitude is impossible. We approve the presence of missionaries in all lands or we do not. Our friends speak pleasantly and hopefully about them or they do not. They cannot now be let alone, and it is well that they come under the fire of criticism and examination.

I

(*a*) Some criticism is mean and malicious and can be instantly dismissed. Men who do not care for the good of others have no standing in this court. Men with selfish interests to serve, who would rather deal with an ignorant and uncivilized group than with their equals, are of no importance as critics of missions. The only damage they do, and it is real damage, is in making missionary believers restive and fretful under criticism and analysis prompted by no such sordid motives.

(*b*) Some criticism arises from ignorance or disapproval of the actual purpose and programme of the enterprise. When a man does not know what you are trying to do, he can hardly be expected to estimate fairly the way you are doing it. And if he should not agree fundamentally with what you are trying to do, he inevitably becomes your critic all along the line.

(*c*) Some criticism arises out of ignorance of the actual state of the enterprise. The early practice, in discussing " heathen " lands, was to standardize a whole nation by its worst specimens or practices. A natural reaction is the current practice of standardizing a nation by the exceptional best that is known. The first practice said, " Since this evil custom is prevalent, the whole social life is evil." The second practice says, " Since this good fact, or this excellent person is real, there cannot be anything radically wrong with the social order of the nation." There is not much to choose between these two. The same bad practices have been in vogue in the discussion of missions.

When critics say that missionaries ought to do this or that, it is always possible to discover for them missionaries who are doing just what they say, though others may not be doing it. The whole enterprise cannot be judged by either group. It is often difficult to accept a criticism and apply it where it belongs, because it is not fair to the enterprise as a whole. This is an inevitable price which the missionary movement must pay for its vast dimensions. Anything can be true of it somewhere. Chapter and verse can be given for virtually any charge laid against it. The serious question is not whether the criticism is true in a given instance, but whether it rests on wide knowledge of the facts and proceeds from a sincere agreement with the fundamental purposes of the movement. Some proposals for the " improvement " of the enterprise would wreck it because they conflict with any sound missionary idea.

(d) One goes on to say gladly that some criticism of the missionary movement proceeds from utmost sympathy and sincere desire to see its main

ends served. It may be stated in ways that do dire
damage, magnifying some detail into illogical importance, centering attention on instances rather
than main currents and taking isolated events as
indications of prevailing conditions. But every
great enterprise, as it grows greater, calls for more
and more searching and severe examination. It
should be self-examination; if that does not come,
then it must come from without.

II

No Christian work is under more frequent and
sincere self-examination than this missionary movement. Its workers and responsible leaders are in
frequent and earnest discussion about its many
details and fundamental issues. Yet close proximity to so great a work may hinder clear judgment
regarding it. Therefore it is well that others speak
their minds freely and that they be accepted not as
foes but as sincere friends who do not wish the
nerve of missions cut. It is well to heed any warn-
ing they may give that this or that condition tends
to cut that nerve.

Indeed, the very vastness of the enterprise is a
natural ground of criticism. Vigorous Chinese opposition to missionary educational work grew of
the revelation of the wide extent and great variety
of these educational plants and programmes by a
commission on Christian Education in China, led
by President Burton, of Chicago University, in

1921. American observers are often surprised at
the figures of personnel and finance now involved
in the missionary movement. They do not measure
it against the strength of the churches which supply
the men and the money nor against the need which
this personnel and finance must supply. The Chinese critics did not measure the missionary educational programme against the immense and utterly
unsupplied need in China. These uninformed
Americans often miss entirely the purpose of so
large an enterprise, as, again, the Chinese missed
the purpose of missionaries. In both cases they
think in terms of some sort of dominion or domination rather than of mere helpfulness.

In his *Novum Organum*, I, 199, Francis Bacon
wrote a needed word on this matter:

It will not be amiss to distinguish the three kinds,
and as it were grades, of ambition in mankind: The
first is of those who desire to extend their power in
their native country; which kind is vulgar and degener-
ate. The second is of those who labour to extend the
power of their country and its dominion among men;
this certainly has more dignity but not less covetous-
ness. But if a man endeavour to establish and extend
the power and dominion of the human race over the
universe, his condition is without doubt both a wholesome thing and a nobler thing than the other two.

Intelligent observers of foreign missions need not
be told that the third and " wholesome and noble "
thing is what the enterprise is trying to accomplish.

But if one feared that the ambition really took either of the other forms, his criticism of the movement would be inevitable. Here is the most widespread enterprise consciously carried on by humanity today, touching more of life, reaching into wider areas, dealing with more situations, than any other. It needs to be understood before it is criticized, but also it ought to welcome all criticisms and tests.

Four questions are always in order regarding the missionary movement:
1. What is the Church trying to do; that is, what is its Aim?
2. Why is it trying to do it; that is, what is its Motive?
3. How is it trying to do it; that is, what are its Methods?
4. How is it getting on; that is, what is the Present Situation?

Confusion or ignorance about any one of these four questions will involve criticism and mistaken judgment.

(a) Many phrases have been used to state succinctly the real aim of missions. Let this be considered:

The missionary movement is the effort of Christian believers to make Jesus Christ known in all the world so that men everywhere may become His followers and His spirit and principles may be applied to the whole of life.

This latter part involves a long process. Some observers feel that the *missionary* element in the total Christian movement should be confined to the first part of the " aim," leaving the rest of it for the believers in each land. The Christian faith itself, however, does not fall into such separate sections. No sooner are men won to Christ than they begin to realize the necessity for applying His spirit and principles to the whole of their life and to the social order in which they live.

(*b*) Yet nothing can take the place of the effort to win more men to Christ's discipleship. The world needs, above all other things just now, for its social and moral order an increased number of men in all nations who take their relation to Christ seriously—more Christian believers and better ones. In many lands this is keenly felt. Christian leaders in Japan and China, in the opening of the conflict of early 1932, deplored the fact that they simply had not enough Christians to bring right and helpful influences to bear on the situation. The actual " converting " of men into sincere Christian discipleship can never be replaced by proposals of an eclectic faith in which each man would merely improve his present religious position. This will be discussed in later chapters of this book. All that is here urged is that the task of missions can never omit either the winning of men to Christ or the applying of Christ's spirit and principles to the whole of life.

(*c*) Lower, and even more popular, " aims " will emerge in our discussion of motives. Our main concern now is whether present conditions suggest change in the motives which should, or actually do, dominate the enterprise. Christian people can hardly question whether it will be well to accomplish the suggested " aim." This would be to doubt the value of Christ to ourselves. If Christ means little to us we will naturally be little concerned that other people should know Him. If He means much to us, we will be concerned that He may mean much to others, and this cannot be until they come to know Him. As a later chapter will point out, it is not necessary to say that other people are all wrong in their present faith, but it will be necessary to say that this faith which has come to us has values for all men that are not otherwise available. It came to us with its freightage of values; it seems only reasonable that it should go from us to others with the same freightage.

II

HAS THE MISSIONARY MOTIVE BEEN MODIFIED?

MISSIONARY motives are many and varied. Large bodies of men do not have the same motives in following the same general course. Why does a man practice medicine? Why does a man teach? Why do people marry? Why do people carry on business? No motive can be named which is so universal that it covers the entire group. Why does the Christian Church seek to make Christ known to all men? Why do young people go out to the mission field? Why do workers remain there? The motives are too many and too varied to be listed.

Still, it can be observed that they fall into three types, as for any great movement or action:

1. There are *fundamental* motives—those which are essential in some form to permanence in the movement, not varying in their actual meaning with changing times or conditions;

2. There are *collateral* motives—those which are modified by the times and conditions under which the work is done, but without disturbing the essential nature of the movement;

3. There are *defective* motives—those which do
not bear the strain of experience, putting a worker
out of line with the real movement, altering its
very essence.

(*a*) These three types occur in all professions,
walks of life, movements of humanity. Men practice medicine, teach, marry, carry on business, go
out as missionaries, for these typical reasons. The
fundamental motives hold the missionary enterprise to its essential purpose, but the failure of defective motives or the variation of collateral ones
often brings the enterprise under suspicion. When
it is said that " the reason for missions has passed,"
it is like the similar saying that " the day of the
pulpit is over." That depends on the real reason
for missions and the real place of the pulpit. Defective motives for missions do " pass," leaving
some workers and supporters adrift or in opposition. Collateral motives do change their shape in
such radical ways that those who have lived by
them are left stranded unless they are able to see
how their substance is retained in new forms. In
critical times one needs to look carefully for the
fundamental motives; have they changed or not?

(*b*) In all great movements or actions the fundamental motives seem chimerical and pretentious
to some observers. No high-minded physician can
state his deepest reasons for being a physician
without using language which some physicians will
count mere rhetoric. Much current literature on

marriage scoffs at the supposedly fundamental reasons for marriage. In some circles it is not counted intelligent to claim that the motives of the Great War were really fine and sacrificial.

In mission lands as well as in sending countries it is incredible to some observers that the fundamental motives of missionaries are their real motives. If a man cannot feel the push of high reasons himself, he will count it affectation for another man to claim these reasons. When a speaker in a mission land was asked contemptuously by a hearer where were his credentials from his imperialistic government, and simply laughed, saying that his government had no knowledge whatever of his being there or of his message, the hearer refused to accept any such word, insisting that " desire to do good to others " was only a pretence among normal human beings. A father came to the head of a mission school to ask what the teacher would pay him for sending his son to the school. The teacher explained that it would be the other way around; the father would have to pay. To this the father demurred. The teacher would gain all the " merit " of instructing his son; where did the father get anything for it? The motive of personally disinterested service was beyond him and he could not credit it in any one. This underlies the wide suspicion that missionaries are the " advance agents " of imperialistic governments, and that converts are their " running dogs." Missionaries are blamed for not having prevented this misunderstanding, but the difficulty lies in the whole philosophy of life which they have encountered. Some people in the home lands are mystified by the entire enterprise, trying to explain it in any way except the natural one of accepting the proposed fundamental motives as the real ones.

I

1. *Since this is a Christian movement, the fundamental motive must be somehow connected with Christ.* In all its forms it is so connected.

(*a*) Often this is found in His command to carry His message everywhere and to secure disciples and train them in His teaching. There can be no serious question that He did so command and that the duty of a servant is to obey. The " Iron Duke " Wellington counted it a species of treason to raise a question about missionary work after that fact became clear. If Christ orders it, how shall a Christian discuss it?

> Theirs not to make reply,
> Theirs not to reason why;
> Theirs but to do—and die.

But as a matter of fact this is not meant to have the force in the Christian spirit that some declare. Blind and unreasoning obedience doubtless has its place in human life under stress of serious peril. The captain of a sinking ship has right of life and death over all passengers and crew, and can order action which must be taken without argument. When a surgeon is in the midst of a critical operation he must be obeyed on the instant by all attendants; there is no room for discussion or question. When a soul knows itself lost and hears Christ speak the word of command, there is no time for quibbles; only obedience is logical.

Yet this is not Christ's way with His followers. His commands are never arbitrary, arising only out of His power and right to order them. He demands that men come to Him with their minds at their best. We are servants of a rational Master, all of whose reasons we cannot hope to know but enough of whose reasons come to us to give us sense of rational action. We need only observe any command of Christ to feel that we are in the presence of the highest reason. The spread of Christian truth would have been as clearly our duty if He had never commanded it as it is now. He commanded what any thoughtful man can see is the only logical and reasonable thing to do. Christ is our Master, but He does not ask for obedience merely for the sake of obedience. Instead, He directs us into fields of service worthy of our best effort, worthy of Himself.

(b) The fundamental motive for Christian missions rests in the logic of Christ Himself—His life and His teaching. His teaching could not be true anywhere if it were not also true everywhere. He does not present mere aspects of truth to be compared with other aspects and accepted or rejected as alternatives. He requires a world setting. What He is for any race, He is suited to become to all races. An article by President Henry Sloane Coffin which appeared in *The Christian Century* for January 14, 1931, phrases this fact:

It is this cosmic setting of the figure of Jesus which compels Christians to attempt to spread His authority over all peoples. He belongs to a whole world, and a whole world belongs to Him. This seems unintelligible and arrogant to those who are not His followers. . . . But from the beginning, those who have found the lordship of Jesus the source of new life have found it impossible not to share Him with all men. And such sharing has never meant that Jesus was to be placed along with other spiritual leaders in men's reverent regard. He never can divide a soul's allegiance with others. Wherever Jesus becomes a force in human life, He takes an exclusive supremacy. . . . How can it be otherwise when men find in Him the God they adore—the disclosure of the controlling spirit of the universe?

In the same spirit the Message of the Jerusalem Conference centres all the missionary movement upon Christ:

Our message is Jesus Christ. . . . The Gospel is not our discovery or achievement; it rests on what we recognize as an act of God. It is first and foremost " good news." It announces glorious truth. Its very nature forbids us to say that it may be the right belief for some but not for others. Either it is true for all or it is not true at all.

Even the details of Christ's teaching involve this. For example, His idea of God cannot be true for one group of men while other men rightly think of God in some lower and less worthy way. If that truth about God—His love and His care for men, His holy character and Fatherly nature, His wish to be known and loved in return—if that truth changes the world outlook of any men, it would do so for all men, and those who have experienced it could not fail to wish the same experience for other men.

His teaching about man is equally universal. That teaching puts a valuation on every man which is sorely needed in our own day. One current writer against missions remarks that the whole Christian theory breaks down on the failure of humanity to justify the high expectations of Christ. Men are not worth as much as the Christian faith implies. Many cynical voices say similar things. James Branch Cabell asks:

What is man? An ape who chatters to himself of kinship with arch-angels while filthily he digs for ground-nuts;

While Henry L. Mencken declares that

Man is a sick fly taking a dizzy ride on a gigantic wheel. He is lazy, improvident and unclean.

But a more thoughtful voice sounds a worthier note

regarding " certain great convictions " which have
sustained Western civilization for one hundred and
fifty years.   Vernon L. Parrington, in *Main Currents in American Thought,* says:

Faith in the excellence of man, in the law of progress,
in the ultimate reign of justice, in the conquest of
nature, in the finality and sufficiency of democracy;
faith, in short, in the excellence of life, was the great
driving force. . . . Faith in machinery came to super-
sede faith in man. . . . And now we have fallen so low
that our faith in justice, progress, the potentialities of
human nature, the excellence of democracy, is stricken
with pernicious anemia and our faith in the machine
is dying.

Over against all this the missionary enterprise sets
the highest possible estimate of humanity.   Though
it lays heavy stress on its offer of redemption in
Christ, it despairs of no man and of no race.   If
men hold other races in contempt, they will make
no effort to bring to them the blessings of redemption and civilization.   If, however, they think of
other men as having equal rank with themselves,
dear to the same God, endowed with the same
spiritual powers, open to the same influences from
God, then there is no escape from the logic of
missions.

There is no single teaching of Jesus which does
not involve the same universality.

(*c*) Relation to Christ produces a spirit, best
described as a love, for Himself and, on His ac-

count, for other men. Something about Him makes His followers want to do something for other people. It is a phenomenon which deserves study. When a fine, sacrificial thing needs to be done it looks to all observers entirely logical for a Christian to do it. If he does not do it, his failure is generally excused on the ground that the demand was more than human nature would endure. But when he does yield to the demand and does some especially fine deed of sacrifice for people who have no direct claim on him, then he is used as an argument for the fineness of human nature, to show how high human nature can rise. This means that the impulse to love and sacrifice which Jesus forms in men is no violation of their natures but is rather a drawing out of their finest traits.

This becomes not only an impulse but also a standard for the work attempted. So it is put by Bishop Linton of Persia, an active missionary, in *International Review of Missions,* January, 1931:

We are out for service, Christian service, and whether it be in our schools or hospitals or welfare centres, or in any other sphere, we aim at giving the best we have. We believe that we have no excuse as missionaries for offering less than our best in educational or medical work. Just because it is done in the name of our Master we want it to be a credit to His name. This, too, is our justification for evangelism; the Gospel which we preach is the best we know. We believe we have had an experience in Jesus Christ which has been to us as life from the dead. We are compelled to share it.   Hence we aim to make every activity of life evangelistic.   We fail badly.   We know that. But in spite of our failure we persist in keeping this before us as our aim.

" We are out for service;" that is the clue to the whole movement.   It is of the genius of being a Christian that this should be true.

Much is said about the value of " sharing our best with others " as a motive in missions.   We need to observe that unless this desire is connected with essential religious experience it does not work out into abiding missionary impulse.   Everybody, non-Christian as well as Christian, has some things which he counts the " best," but how many feel an impulse to take pains to share them with others? If this were an independent motive, we might expect to find large numbers of movements which would carry men and women over the seas to " share their best with others."   Unhappily we do not find these movements except in connection with a sense of Christ or some gift of His as the " best " that is to be shared.   If any one sets out on the errand of missions without that " best " to give, he soon finds that the general desire to " share his best with others " fades away under pressure of the hard realities of human life.   It is only under the drive of religion that this becomes dominant.   For Christian believers it is part of that striking phenomenon of a new spirit of service which seems born of relation to Christ.

All this is a mere expansion of the one fact that *the fundamental motive of the missionary movement is connected directly with relation to Christ*. Conditions or special times cannot alter that motive. Why should a Christian believer come to think differently unless more richly of God or of man or of right conduct or of right relations of men to each other and to God? Do seasons or geography or forms of government or international relations change this? The motive will find varied expression and it may take on unusual forms, but the central fact in it will not be changed. The nerve of missions is not cut while this motive abides.

II

2. The collateral motives are many. They are all good in their place and to some degree, but they are liable to change, even to disappear. If observers identify their existence with the particular forms they have taken in history they may count the nerve of the enterprise cut when these motives are radically altered. A full list will be impossible, but a few may be named as illustrations of what is meant.

(*a*) A powerful motive is found in accent on some form of human " loss," with the consequent impulse to save one's fellow-men from it. So powerful is the motive that those who feel its drive cannot believe that the enterprise can be carried

forward without it. And without doubt there can
be little incentive to bring a Gospel of salvation to
men who do not need it. The entire issue is as to
the nature of the " loss " which will be accented.
That men are now " lost " in very vital and awe-
some sense is obvious to anybody who will look
around him, doubly clear to any one who will look
at the nations of the world who have not known
Christ. That this " loss " extends to a permanent
alienation from God is the haunting dread and
concern of many who support the missionary movement. But undoubtedly the assurance of permanent and eternal " loss " is less vivid in our day
than it formerly seemed to be. Many feel that the
dimming of this assurance has cut the nerve of missions. Unless we are saving men from eternal loss,
why bother about them? Anything less seems like
a mere programme for improving temporal conditions, and it is urged that this will never inspire
sacrifice in living or in giving. How much truth
there is in this any observer knows. There are
many earnest men who would lose their concern for
these millions without Christ if they felt that their
eternal state was dependent on anything else than
someone's faithfulness in proclaiming the gracious
love of God in Christ. Earnest missionary leaders
declare that until we can bring back into Christian
consciousness the assurance of hell and the destiny
of eternal condemnation for all those who do not
know and accept the Christ of history we shall not

recover the passion for missions. For them this is not a collateral motive but a fundamental one.

The issue here is not one of fact but of the place which the fact of the future must have in the motive of Christian missions. It does serve in many lives to make the essential value of Christ so much the more vivid. If, however, this essential value can be demonstrated in any one's mind by other means, then the fact of the future can be left unused in the impulse to make Him known. The Jerusalem Council expressed it in this way:

We believe that men are made for Christ and cannot really live apart from Him. Our fathers were impressed with the horror that men should die without Christ—we share that horror; we are impressed also with the horror that men should live without Christ. . . . We cannot live without Christ and we cannot bear to think of men living without Him. We cannot be content to live in a world that is un-Christlike. We cannot be idle while the yearning of His heart for His brethren is unsatisfied.

Dr. Griffith John, the notable China missionary, discussed this question at length and insisted that the eternal destiny of men was not essential to his missionary impulse, while he shared the awe and fear of the fact itself. The point just now is that this is a motive which may or may not actuate a missionary worker. It is subject to alteration and new accent by the conditions under which the ministry is performed. There can be no doubt of the "loss" of men this very day. Some, the writer among them, see no escape from the logic that carries that fact on out into the eternity to which we are all going. If others find escape from that logic or refuse to accede to it, they may still feel the irresistible drive of their own experience with Christ and their sense of His will which will carry them to the service of men everywhere. It is not the form of the " loss " that matters; it is the fact of " loss " biting in upon one's heart of compassion. Eternal results may be left, indeed must be left, to the unfailing wisdom and love of God. As Griffith John once said, we know that by our preaching and living men do find God in Christ; whether the gracious Holy Spirit of God, who " worketh when and where and how He pleaseth " has ways of dealing with earnest souls beyond our preaching, we may leave to Him. A very earnest and successful missionary pastor expressed in a conference his entire dissent from the implications of these familiar lines:

> Let none whom He has ransomed fail to greet Him,
>   Through thy neglect unfit to see His face.

He contended that no man's eternal destiny could depend in God's purpose on another man's actions, but must depend on each man's relation to Christ. There is no other means of salvation but in Christ, but how the eternal Christ is mediated to the souls of men we gladly leave to God, rejoicing to know that He is certainly mediated through our feeble preaching. The motive has greater or less power without altering the project itself.

(b) Another collateral motive is found in the desire to extend our form of civilization or some of its benefits to people less fortunate than ourselves —education, social customs, commerce, housing, lighting, and the like. First contact with people of other cultures naturally brings to light the conditions which differ from ours; if these seem defective or hurtful, we incline to set our own over against them. Much early missionary argument dealt with these adverse differences. We accented the poverty, the disease, the ignorance, the savagery, the injustice of the nations to whom it was intended that missionaries go. William Carey felt that he was going down into a pit and asked his brethren to hold the ropes for him. The representation was perfectly true and the words of early ·missionaries can be sustained by abundant fact. All these evils did exist, and many of them exist widely still, all of them in some parts of the world.

The motive tends to lose force as the work goes on. We come to realize more clearly that Western ways—our education, housing, social forms—are not unmitigated blessings even to ourselves, and our new friends adopt some things which we wish we could ourselves abandon. We find also that alongside the evils in their society which challenged our attention at first, there are excellent practices and conditions which we would not wish changed,

which we might even imitate to our advantage.
The social life of non-Christian nations is not all
bad, the customs are not all evil, the relationships
among men are not all so crude as we thought at
first.   Moreover, we find these other nations over-
taking us with their own programmes of education
and culture and commerce.   They may even dislike
our ways as different from their own.   They adopt
what we teach and presently work out what suits
them better, whether we like it or not.   So, China
sets up its own educational system and demands
that we accede to it or close our schools!   This is
a real reversal of form.   Japan has established such
rigid medical requirements that some missionary
doctors cannot register.   What was once so needed
in education and medicine and industry seems no
longer required.   It may prove so in agriculture,
just now occupying a more adequate share of missionary attention.   We can do so well that presently we will become unnecessary.   This ought to
be our desire.

But this obviously alters the force of the motive
for spreading in all the world the benefits of our
civilization and discovery.   Our Western science is
wonderful, but people in mission lands in their own
laboratories are making discoveries which write
their names high on the list with the best of our
own.

Let us not go astray here.   Most of the world is
pitifully lacking in the things that make our West-

ern life easier and more pleasant. There are woeful ignorance, distressing diseases wholly unrelieved, crude methods of farming which leave whole populations on the verge of starvation when there might be plenty, hurtful social practices, injustice to women and little children, oppressive codes of human faith and conduct—all this and much more. The motive of extending the benefit of civilization is vital and valid. All that is now urged is that if it should be found to be no longer operative in a given case, the missionary enterprise is not affected even in that case, since attention will shift to some other forms of need, probably even deeper than those already relieved. Missionary work is not discredited when one meets cultured gentlemen and attractive women from " mission lands " and find that their mode of living is not savage nor crude. The missionary argument is not ended when travellers return from port cities or from flying visits to selected places in mission lands with reports of pleasant conditions they found there. Such stories " cut the nerve of missions " for those only who were moved by a collateral motive and could not read its meaning in large terms. " Mission lands " have much yet to learn from the lands which Christ has blessed, but it may not be electric light and automobiles and sewing machines that are needed.

(c) Another collateral motive for missions is found in the spirit of " adventure for Christ." Professor McTaggart, for some strange reason,

feared that Christ's programme would make tame
people if it were really followed.   This is by no
means the impression He makes on most observers.
He set out on a campaign which knew no limits.
From a tiny land which was a kind of cross-roads
for the nations, He proposed a world-wide conquest
through spiritual forces.   He braved social opposition, religious denunciation, personal suffering, for
the sake of carrying on His project.   To a great
many people the most daring thing they can do is
to attempt to follow Him.   Professor Rauschen-
busch thought the real question is, " Dare We Be
Christians? "

The motive of adventure " for " or " with "
Christ is a powerful one with many people.   Life
is always a great adventure, but few people can
maintain the adventurous spirit in the long, slow
grind of carrying on when conditions are adverse.
For instance, it is a great adventure to rear children, setting new lives into right paths, moulding
energies for the future.   But there come times in
the rearing of a family when the sheer monotony
and grind of getting things done as they have to be
done robs the whole task of its adventure; novelty
is gone, the spring is lost from both step and spirit.
Yet the work has to be done, and if there is not a
deeper and more lasting motive than adventure,
one's courage oozes out and one wishes it could
somehow be ended, and that is fatal to any great
undertaking.   In all adventures there are periods

of sag and tameness when one must drive on for some other reason than the adventure.

So in missionary work. It is altogether possible at certain points and under certain conditions to leap to it with all the joy of a great exploration. Christ is projecting a great world programme for human good and for release of men from oppression and evil. It is no wonder that eager souls leap to it, choosing rather to fail with Christ than to succeed with any one else, preferring to go down to wreck in a brave attempt than to live on placidly doing nothing of any importance. We have too little of this in the Christian life. The timid way in which many parents approach the matter and their tearful refusal to allow their sons and daughters to enter missionary service because it might be difficult for them and might even cost them their lives, shows how far we are generally from the spirit of adventure. When young people appear with this motive they should be encouraged. They need also to be reminded that this is a long drawn out process with its rough places as well as its inspiring marches toward victory. The movement cannot be carried through its trying periods merely as an adventure. The motive is good, but collateral to the essential ones.

(d) More can be said for the motive of " building a world brotherhood " or " extending the Kingdom of God on earth." World strife must be replaced by world peace, and this cannot be done without the spread of a spirit which is found by us Christians only in Christ. To give one's self to the task of spreading that spirit and establishing that brotherhood is worthy the best one has and can do. The Jerusalem Council phrased it well, when it declared:

We believe in a Christlike world. We know nothing better; we can be content with nothing less. We do not go to the nations called non-Christian because they are the worst of the world and they alone are in need—we go because they are part of the world and share with us in the same human need—the need of redemption from ourselves and from sin, the need to have life complete and abundant and to be remade after this pattern of Christlikeness. We desire a world in which Christ will not be crucified but where His spirit shall reign.

Could any one ask better than to be allowed to spend his life working toward such an end? Many elements enter into movements for the making of world peace—commerce, industry, travel—and it is of first importance that a goodly number of religious people shall be as deeply involved as any others. They have more at stake than any others because only such a world can give full swing to the religion which they profess.

At the same time, it must be frankly faced that much actual missionary work seems only remotely connected with so large a movement as that of " world brotherhood." Much of it is prosaic, plodding service which seems as little connected with world conditions as any good work done in America or England. Helping to transform a plain life or a simple village in India or China is a vital part of the missionary movement, but it is related to changing world conditions only by a constant act of faith and imagination. If this should be one's dominating motive in going out to mission work, one must be prepared for disillusionment such as overtakes any one who sets out on a large errand and finds he has to deal with recalcitrant and remote elements or that much of his work is at long remove from the supposed end. It is a sustaining motive but it will not bear the strain of regular normal missionary experience. Nothing too strong can be said about it, for it deserves all praise from thoughtful men. But it cannot carry so great a movement as that of missions in its daily activities.

(e) Similar word must be said about the motive of justifying the validity of religion in human life. The current of secularism is noted everywhere. Religion is at a discount. Yet here is something done under the spur of religion, producing results in the field of religion, revealing the real power of religion, which helps to make reply to those who discount it and consider it an outgrown, outworn experience. For a man to whom religion means a great deal it is a worthy desire to do the thing that will justify it before men, the more if he feels that the largest danger of the world today is its loss of religion.

The motive is valid whenever it is consistently held.   It must include the dangers that are only too evident everywhere from a poor form of religion or from mistaken methods of serving one's own religion.   Fanaticism must be frankly recognized and shown to be an abnormal use of the real values of faith.   But the motive must be connected with that form of religion which the missionary has found worth carrying to the uttermost parts of the earth. It is not the validity of " religion " in some vague and general sense that is proved by the missionary movement, but the validity of the Christian religion, shown in this movement to be of such value that it is worth life and effort.   Probably the rock on which it splits as a forceful motive is that it is so difficult to keep it pure, and also that it leads to efforts that are in some degree matched by men without it, men intent merely on profit and exploration and adventure.   If they do for those poorer motives the same thing that missionaries do under pressure of the religious motive, then religion is not necessarily proved to be valid and desirable any more fully than these other motives.

III

3. There are several defective motives, which will not bear the strain of real missionary work.

(*a*) There is a glamour about the work at a distance which makes the romantic motive operative.   The joy of going to " the poor heathen " who must be so glad to have a Christian come and tell them of Christ and help to change their very bad customs; the romance of living under the primitive and informal conditions of these lands, with savages all about and simple-hearted people open to all suggestions of help; the chance to see the world by travel and to know strange lands; the novelty of other ways of living and different practices in the ordinary ways of human relationship— such things seem trivial when they are worded frankly, but no one knows the first approach of some people to missionary work without knowing that in various forms these motives do emerge. So real are they that many opponents of the enterprise believe them to be the major motives of young people who do actually go. In these days of careful selection of candidates it is unlikely that many recruits go out with palpably defective motives, but even a modicum of this motive is apt to weaken a new missionary at critical points. Almost nothing in this wording of the case represents the real situation on the field, unless possibly the real interest in seeing other lands and other ways of living. But this interest soon dies out. The actual work is utterly unromantic, though some spirits are able to keep its adventurous and romantic elements vital until the very end. A veteran about to retire told a group of young missionaries that unless the work had a glow of romance about it they would not remain on the field, but it was evident that the romance he had found in it was not that which appears from across the sea before one has dealt with the actual situations.

(*b*) Equally defective, but more subtle, is the sense of superiority, the spirit of patronizing one's inferiors. Paul once warned early Christians against this, classing them with the more arrogant types among the Jews: " What has thou that thou didst not receive? " What ground for boasting is there when one is a receiver at all times? Many early missionary addresses unconsciously fed this spirit in describing the sad condition of the people of mission lands. Hearers almost inevitably standardized the entire people by the entirely truthful bad instances that were given. It is natural that one should have a patronizing spirit when one goes to the aid of the unfortunate. It appears in much city mission work when a kind-hearted and affluent person tries to help the poor and needy. It appears sometimes in missionaries, when they lose their sense of dependence on what they themselves receive. They may act as though what they are offering is their personal benefaction, instead of realizing that they are mere messengers of Christ who is the whole reason for their having anything to give.

This motive roots in a real condition. Obviously, unless one has something better to offer than the people have, it is impertinent and may be insulting to go to them. If a missionary did not believe that the faith which has come to him is better, richer, more satisfying than the faith which it is to supplant, he would surely not be there at all. This feeds in some people the sense of personal arrogance, as though they themselves were superior and ought to be so recognized. The motive breaks down in most lands, where the people do not admit that the newcomer has any advantage over themselves. In appearance, practice, religion, he is often counted merely odd and strangely misguided. When he discovers that fact, this defective motive fails him.

(c) This is why any sense of self-sacrifice is dangerous on the mission field. The people who love their own country do not see any sacrifice in a person leaving any other land for it; the missionary lives well from their point of view; he travels; he uses servants; he goes about in as much ease as they themselves do; the food he eats is not so good as theirs, but he chooses it, and there is no accounting for tastes except that some tastes, such as his, are peculiar. No, a missionary reveals no sacrifice to the average national in any mission land. A returned student from America to one of the mission lands explained that he had never felt the slightest appreciation of the presence of missionaries until he had been in America and had seen how people lived there; then he knew what sacrifice had occurred. Missionaries cannot use it as a motive because it is simply wasted on the people.

The only real reason for considering these defective motives is that observers who do not understand the work suppose they are the motives under which the work is done. The slightest serious thought will show how inadequate they are. Unless larger and worthier motives are dominant, the work would have ended long ago. Workers who go to the field with any considerable element of these defective motives are soon at home again, disillusioned and often disgruntled. Things did not turn out as they expected, but their expectations were absurd. When observers learn that the peoples to whom missionaries go are not necessarily inferior socially to many in the home land and that many of them do not want nor welcome the missionaries, they suppose the nerve of missions has been cut. The fact is that such ideas have never been part of the vital nerve of missions. They can all be lost without the slightest damage to the real missionary impulse. Respectable people in any American city need the essential Gospel of Christ, His salvation, His constant aid, as truly as the least cultured in the most neglected areas of the land, and as many of them are apt to reject Him. This may occur in any land.

All the defective motives can be cancelled, any of the collateral motives can be altered or omitted, and the fundamental motives alone can still carry the project. Loss of these fundamental motives will cut the missionary nerve. But these motives are not being lost nor changed by anything in present life.

III

WHAT IS THE EFFECT OF OUR CHANGED ATTITUDE TOWARD OTHER RELIGIONS?

MANY Christian believers and missionary supporters have changed their attitude toward other religions, though all have not done so. The classification of one religion as wholly true and all others as wholly false, a classification not at all restricted to Christians, has given place to a recognition of the witness of God to Himself in all sincere faiths and of the possibility of error in some forms of any religion. As to Christianity, Romanists have long felt this about Protestantism and certainly Protestants have felt it about Romanism. It is no longer defensible for an adherent of any one religion to think of himself as wholly right while others are wholly wrong. Does that fact cut the nerve of missionary effort?

I

In the midst of many variations, and with many more groups of local standing, there are five "great" religions. In the order of their appearance they are:

43

1. Hinduism, dating before recorded history;
2. Judaism, taking definite form about 1500 B. C.;
3. Buddhism, about 550 B. C.;
4. Christianity, furnishing our date-line;
5. Islam (Mohammedanism), A. D. 422.

Beside these are forms of religion such as Parseeism or Zoroastrianism (660 B. C.), Confucianism (600 B. C.), Shinto peculiar to Japan, undated, (B. C.), Sikhism (A. D. 1468), and a large number of cults and schisms. Each of these must, in the nature of the case, claim something peculiar and essential for those who adhere to it. Each has variations so wide that adherents of one group may deny the right of another group to claim the name at all. This comes from the natural and desirable trait of personal freedom in the field of relation to God and spiritual realities.

The issue now is as to the attitude which sincere adherents of one faith should take toward other faiths. The " greatness " of a religion is not measured by the number of its adherents. Once each of these faiths had a very small following; numerical tests would have ruled it out. But a religion is adherently true or not, whatever following it has. Yet of course there is argument in the fact that large numbers of sincere men find religious satisfaction in a particular faith, and the argument grows as the number increases. Christian believers cannot be indifferent to the fact that their faith has now become the most widespread among men. This does not prove it to be true, but it adds weight to other arguments.

II

Dr. Karl Reischauer speaks of five attitudes toward other religions: Opposition, indifference, over-appreciation, cold-blooded and scientific appraisal, sympathetic insight.   He adds that " Christians can afford to be generous."

For our purposes it may be well to consider four attitudes which have marked Christian believers in their thought of other faiths:

1. Indifference.   Missionary work is to be carried on without reference to other faiths; they are negligible, neither to be attacked nor studied. When a missionary sent back to his home society an analytical study of the religion of the land where he was stationed, his society wrote him that he was not there to spend his time on such things; he was to replace the religion, whatever it might be, and it did not matter what it is.   The writer of an excellent study of the original faiths of his mission field, published in 1932, explains in his preface that this work has been done in vacations and leisure hours, and has not been allowed to displace any missionary efforts; he knows there are some who would wonder that a missionary would take time for the study of " native " faiths.   Of course there is merit in this position from one point of view.   If one is

deeply and adequately served by his own faith, he
need not be forever investigating other faiths to see
if there is anything better. The average Christian
does not need to study Islam and Hinduism since
Christ has satisfied his own heart. Missionaries
find a deep unrest the world around, and the first
service they render is not the disturbing of quiet
hearts, but the quieting of disturbed hearts. Sometimes, to be sure, unrest needs to be created, if an
adherent has lost his real concern for the service of
religion and does not realize how far his own is
failing him.

But this attitude of indifference is not worthy of
the Christian spirit. Here are multitudes of men
whom God loves and to whom Christ is sent, and
they all think something about God and about the
way of dealing with sin and sorrow and about the
way of living with each other and about eternity.
How can it be a matter of indifference to those who
want to show them the better way, what it is that
they believe and practice? Yet there are some who
are so habituated to this attitude of indifference
that any real interest in other religions seems a
surrender of the unique values of the Christian
faith and hence to cut the nerve of missionary zeal.

2. A second attitude is that of intolerance.
These religions are no religions at all; they are
" Satanic devices to deceive men;" there is only
one true religion, the others are to be destroyed and
forgotten. This is not at all confined to Christian

thinking. The Allahabad (India) *Leader* of November 15, 1931, described in an editorial an address by Sri Devamitta Dharmapala, founder of a Buddhist Society, as " an intolerant address," because the speaker " impartially attacked Hinduism, Christianity and Islam and extolled Buddhism at the expense of these great religions." It added that " the intolerance of spirit which this betrayed may do credit to his missionary zeal," but that it bore no promise of success in commending Buddhism to the people of India. On the contrary, said the editorial, the divine message of the Gita " is meant for the whole world, for Hindus of all classes, for the Buddhists, too, and for everyone seeking spiritual advancement."

In its milder form this attitude produces a genuine fear that any real appreciation of other faiths must mean a lessened approval of the Christian faith and so must cut the nerve of missionary effort. This fear led to some unrest in Europe as the Jerusalem Council approached and at one time it threatened to divide the forces of that gathering. Dr. John R. Mott, who was Chairman of the Jerusalem Council, writing afterward in *The Present-Day Summons to the World Mission of Christianity*, refers to the feeling that if we knew the best of other faiths we might not feel the need for making Christ known everywhere.

It was to meet this very questioning [he says] that the plan used in the preparation of the papers, as well as in their consideration before Jerusalem and in the discussion at Jerusalem, was adopted and carried out. What was the result? It was overwhelmingly proved that the more open-minded, honest, just, and generous we were in dealing with the non-Christian faiths, the higher Christ loomed in His absolute uniqueness, sufficiency, supremacy and universality. More than ever before, we saw Him as One other than all the rest— other than the saints and sages of ancient Hinduism, other than Buddha, Confucius, and Mohammed, other than Moses and St. Paul—" strong among the weak, erect among the fallen, believing among the faithless, clean among the defiled, living among the dead." In all the many months of fresh study of the values of non-Christian systems across the world, or the comprehensive and luminous sharing of knowledge, spiritual insight and personal experience at Jerusalem, nothing was discovered or took place which could tend in the least to invalidate the claim and belief that in Christ we have the Central Figure of the Ages and the Eternities, the Fountain-head of Spiritual Life, the unfailing Source of Creative Energy, the World's Redeemer, the Desire of all Nations.

A meeting was arranged in Cairo where the whole matter was discussed and it was shown that there was no reason for intolerance on the part of missionaries toward the faiths which they met in the field.

But there are still missionary advocates who fear this outcome and who earnestly believe that no tolerance should be shown to other faiths. The fact that some of the most earnest advocates of the Christian faith are also the best informed students of other faiths and rejoice to find witness of God borne in them, should be an answer to this fear. It is no essential missionary attitude to be intolerant of other religions.

3. A third attitude is that of indiscrimination. It is sometimes called tolerance; often it is mere indifference to moral values; but it involves acceptance of all religions as equally good and all faulty. The attitude is common among those who think of certain faiths as good for one locality or one race while others are better for other races and places. An eminent lecturer in Siam during the early part of this century declared: " Our religion is suitable for the country as we observe it, but not for China; therefore the Chinese have modified it. . . . The same is true of other religions. The Europeans hold the Christian religion because it is suitable for their country and their national characteristics. He expressed his conviction that " in essentials it [Christianity] did not differ from Buddhism. Whatever was in Christianity was in Buddhism; they differ only in non-essentials." Still, in ethics, " Our religion [Buddhism] is better than Christianity. And I believe that Jesus learned from Buddha the moral precepts that He taught." On the other hand, he told his hearers that " Moses must have been a Brahmin familiar with the sacred writings." In similar vein later writers on Islam have urged that the Arabs and Turks are Mohammedans, that no

plan should be made to change that fact. Professor Hocking, in his *The Spirit of World Politics*, quotes Khalil Nimat, professor of logic in the University of Stamboul, as saying:

Islam is the religion of the Turkish people. It satisfies the will-to-believe of the individual. It lifts him to a sense of communion with the eternal being. It has the character of true universality. And in its purity it has no official institutions, but imparts its eternal and holy being and its holy injunctions to the consciences of men.

This attitude logically held will doubtless cut the nerve of missions. Why take another defective faith to a world already well supplied with defective faiths? If all religions teach the same thing in different forms, each suited to the section where it is accepted, why present merely another form of the teaching?

With this there arises a peculiar eagerness to find likenesses between or among faiths. If the figure " three " occurs anywhere with reference to God, it is accepted as " the effort of all religions " to teach something like the Trinity. If any stories have grown about the founder of a faith which involved an unusual origin, this is taken as showing how a Virgin Birth is " common to all faiths." If a sacred meal occurs elsewhere, this is the origin of the Lord's Supper. Careless readers of *The Golden Bough* have gone to extremes here, as Sir James Frazer himself did not do. Some likenesses or

similarities bear witness to the fundamental realities of religion as they work out anywhere, but they
indicate no dependence of one faith on another.
Moreover, when religions stand side by side for
years each is apt to show signs of the influence of
the other, the more forceful and aggressive naturally wielding the heavier influence. Thus, there is
no doubt that the coming of Christianity into close
relation with Buddhism has hastened the development of Buddhist ideas of a personal God and of
divine mercy, both lacking in its earliest forms.

There arises here also the vague opinion that religions are pretty much matters of taste or feeling
and that each group is best served by what it likes
best. But religion does not move in the realm of
taste and judgment alone. In this realm very
different ideas may be equally correct because of
different standards. Art and music cannot have
absolute standards; they are matters of taste and
judgment. Chinese art and music are not pleasing
to some in the West, but one could not count them
wrong or mistaken. So with governmental forms.
Of course some governmental systems work out
into evil and cannot be defended, even if their subjects approve them. But it cannot be argued that
all men should have the same form of government.

Religion, however, moves in the realm of fact
and truth, not of opinion and preferences. Two
men may estimate the meaning of a fact differently,
but the fact remains as it is. If one man thinks of

the earth as a flat surface rather than as a sphere, he thinks wrongly and it is not intolerant to say so. One may be very gentle with the error, but it cannot be treated as a mere modification of the truth. If one thinks that the Chinese constitute the majority of the people on the earth, it is nothing to get excited over, but it is not true, and it is not intolerant to take another position.

And if one thinks that God consists of some millions of beings in the spiritual world, thus denying His loving Fatherhood and unity, it is unworthy of Him to denounce the erroneous believers, but it is also unworthy to accept the idea as true equally with the teaching of Christ. If one thinks that the way to win God's love and favour is the way of the " holy men " of India, one can be pitiful and appreciative of the deep sincerity that marks many of them, but it is no intolerance to set the truth of Christ over against the wrong idea in hope that the truth will overcome the error. If one thinks that humanity has no personal immortality and that its destiny is to be blotted out, then one who accepts Christ cannot count this equally true with the assurance of personal immortality.

There is nothing unusual about this. Chemists do not hold that water consists of certain elements in America, but may consist of any number of other elements in other lands. Physicists do not count the electronic theory good in the West but quite uncertain in the East. Physicians do not consider aconite poisonous in England but a healthy diet for Asia. Grant one world, one human race, one God, and the ground is laid for one faith which will include all the values of all faiths but will remain itself.

Religions simply are not equally true. Humanity is better for adherence to some religions than to some others, and by the same logic would be better for adherence to the one which carries the largest guidance to truth. It is not intolerance to say so and to act on the assurance. The method of acting must be worthy of the faith which the programme is meant to offer to the world, but it must be aggressive and earnest. The Joseph Cook lecturer of 1931-32, Rev. Dr. J. Harry Cotton, wrote back from India regarding the oldest faith of the world as follows:

This visit to India has made increasingly clear to me the fact that Christianity can make no peace with Hinduism. No honest visitor can escape the many excellent things in Hindu philosophy and practice. But we went to Benares. There we saw the crudity, the filth, the superstition, and the pathos of Indian faith. The golden temple, which our guide informed us was the most sacred temple of Benares, was crowded with visitors coming from the Ganges where they had bathed to make their offering. Within the temple is no image of any God, but only the phallic symbol, so repeatedly seen in Indian temples. A few days later we sat on the steps of a clean, chaste little temple on the banks of one of the rivers into which the Ganges breaks up before it

pours itself into the Bay of Bengal. We sat on the
steps, watching the river flow by, and talked for two
hours with a monk of the Ramakrishna mission on the
things of the spirit. I was deeply impressed by his
ideals of oneness with God, peace of spirit, and absence
of injury. But then I mentioned what I had seen in
Benares, and the multitudes who were washing there to
have their sins removed. With this he could take no
exception. It was their faith—they could find peace
through those rites. In a later incarnation they might
be born into higher insight. It is this easy-going acqui-
escence with things as they are that so thoroughly con-
demns Hinduism. With this attitude the Gospel of
Christ, with its urgent Gospel of redemption, can make
no peace.

But the option here is no amalgamated faith,
made up of " the best in all faiths." A religious
system is a vital reality if it lives at all. We can no
more replace its parts with sections from other
faiths than we can make a perfect human body by
choosing here a limb, there an eye, and yonder an
ear, each of them pleasing in itself, and hope to
make a living beautiful body out of the collection
of parts. At the Jerusalem Council (Report I, p.
348) a paper was quoted containing the following
suggestive passage:

In so far as the Council could speak for the missionary enterprise and for the Christian Church, both in the
older branches of it and on the mission field, there is to
be no attempt at an amalgamated religion. The missionary enterprise will not be a search for a more ade-

quate and satisfactory religion than Christianity. It
will be the offer of the only Lord and Saviour Jesus
Christ to the whole world and the common effort
of Christian men of all lands and races to explore
and experience His unsearchable riches, infinite and
inexhaustible.

4. The remaining attitude taken by Christian
believers toward other religions is that of intelligent appreciation, with discrimination. It rejoices
in the continuing and unfailing witness of God to
Himself, and finds evidence of His love everywhere. This is the attitude of the Jerusalem
Council and expressed in paragraphs recently so
widely quoted:

We rejoice to think that just because in Jesus Christ
the light that lighteneth every man shone forth in its
full splendour, we find rays of that same light where
He is unknown or even is rejected. We welcome every
noble quality in non-Christian persons or systems as
further proof that the Father, who sent His Son into the
world, has nowhere left Himself without witness. Thus,
merely to give illustration,, and making no attempt to
estimate the spiritual value of other religions to their
adherents, we recognize as part of the one Truth that
sense of the Majesty of God and the consequent rever-
ence in worship, which are conspicuous in Islam; the
deep sympathy for the world's sorrow and unselfish
search for the way of escape, which are at the heart of
Buddhism; the desire for contact with Ultimate Reality
conceived as spiritual, which is prominent in Hinduism;
the belief in a moral order of the universe and consequent insistence on moral conduct, which are inculcated

by Confucianism; the disinterested pursuit of truth and
of human welfare which are often found in those who
stand for secular civilization but do not accept Christ
as their Lord and Saviour.

Such an attitude does not cut the nerve of missions
and yet it is the modern attitude.   It appreciates
all the good in other faiths; it recognizes the sincerity of adherents of those faiths; yet it maintains
assurance of the uniqueness and necessity of Christ
and the Christian faith.

One young minister, writing of rising from his
study of comparative religion, not with his missionary zeal lessened, but with clearer sense of the
place of the Christian faith and its Central Figure,
declares:

My continued philosophical studies are invaluable as
a foundation for my thinking; my continued studies in
comparative religion and history have made me see more
and more the ever-growing uniqueness of Christ Jesus
for my life and for all of life; and my continued love of
the æsthetic, especially in the form of music and poetry,
perpetually kindles the fires of aspiration in my heart,
giving me that vista of eternity and of a God who is
the Inexhaustible One.

As " the cure for the evils of democracy is more
democracy," so the cure for the confusion of the
study of comparative religion is the fuller study of
comparative religion.   The first contact with other
faiths tends to bring out their coarser differences

and this impression is lessened in later study, supplemented by a sense of their values, but this is followed in turn by a deeper sense of their wide difference from the truth of Christ. Surface differences are forgotten in the profounder differences which emerge with further study.

Nothing of this sort cuts the nerve of missionary effort unless an attitude develops which reduces Christ to a level with other religious leaders. Mr. Gandhi said he could not set Christ on a " solitary throne " because there had been many incarnations of God. But it is precisely this " solitary throne " that is claimed for Him by His followers. In urging this solitariness one need not begin with the errors or weaknesses in other faiths which Christ corrects, for it is always open to question whether these evils are inherent in the philosophy of the faith or not. Is caste inherent in Hinduism? Is long-continued transmigration essential to Buddhism? Is the low esteem of womanhood an integral part of Islam? Some observers count them so; others see them disappearing as excrescences, leaving the fundamental religion all the better for the loss. Yet such evils continue today as accepted and defended elements of the religions named, and with them many other evils. If it is said that in Christendom grave evils exist, the reply is that no forces are more constantly opposing these evils than the Christian forces, operating in the name of their religion. This is either not true at all in " mission lands," or else it is only limitedly true.

But the wiser approach to the study of the uniqueness of the Christian faith and its essential nature for the world is by way of its inherent qualities, letting it stand over against the other faiths of the world on its own merits. Many statements have been made in covering these points. The Christian delegates from Japan to the Jerusalem Council brought with them a paper setting forth " the points of superiority of Christianity as compared with other religions," meaning especially Buddhism, Shintoism and Confucianism. It declared:

1. The conception of God as personal, making clear the ethical relation between God and man. 2. Man not seeking to find God but God taking the initiative in seeking for man. Progress not through human effort but through God's condescension. 3. The sense of personality. Respect for individuality and recognition of the absoluteness of the value of personality. 4. Its Scripture, condensed into one volume, can conveniently be carried anywhere and understood by any one. 5. Its superlative ethical sense. Its emphasis on clean living and new advance for the life of every day. Especially does it emphasize the purity of the home. 6. Its stressing of social justice and social service.

In a profounder statement, Dr. John A. Mackay notes three peculiar and essential traits of the Christian faith which other religions do not have. It accents:

1. The transcendent nature of God;
2. The cosmic significance of Christ;
3. The creative approach to Reality.

He adds that " Christ is the present conscience of the world." Moral values and persons are tested by Him and not by others. "Asking why Jesus is put in the highest moral order is like asking why one should say that the sun is the light of the world when we have the moon and stars."

Professor Harnack taught that the great teachings of the Christian faith which gave it power in the early ages are its teaching of

> God the Father as Creator;
> Jesus Christ as Saviour;
> Purity;
> The Resurrection.

Nothing has happened to change the vitality of these nor to displace them, nor are they found in power and clarity outside the Christian faith.*

The whole matter comes back to the uniqueness of Jesus Christ Himself and the incomparable significance of His cross and resurrection. The declaration of the Jerusalem Council already quoted has commanded universal agreement. " Our message is

---

* A further list of seven traits peculiar to the Christian faith is seen in the Author's *The Christian Message and Programme,* Ch. VII: Its Idea of God, of Man, of Salvation; its teaching about Human Society and Human Destiny; its provision of power for the life it requires; its centreing of all on Christ.

Jesus Christ." No other religion has Christ in it—
Christ crucified and risen—and any element in
other religions which suggests Him is re-enforced
and vitalized by fuller presentation of Him. If He
means to His followers what He deserves to mean,
the nerve of their missionary zeal will not be cut by
any kindly thought of other faiths. He will never
inspire hatred or contempt for any other religion or
for the sincere faith of any of those whom He loved
even unto death. He will not encourage His followers to be indifferent to the sincere efforts of
others to follow the path as they see it, but He will
remind them that He is the Way. We cannot follow Him and discount the eagerness of all men to
know the truth, but after all He is the Truth. We
cannot believe in Him and not welcome every sincere effort to live the good life, but we do not forget
that He is the Life. So long as we have Him and
the great realities about God and man and society
and eternity which logically follow from Him we
cannot lose our missionary zeal. We take as our
own the words of a speaker in the assembly of a
missionary college in India, though he was not
himself a Christian believer: "What India needs
today is more men and women, be they Hindu,
Mussalmans or Christians, who know and follow
the teachings of Jesus Christ." The student body,
ninety percent non-Christians, burst into the most
spontaneous applause of the year. As Christians,
we see no hope of following Christ's teachings

without His power. A much loved prince of Siam, shortly before his death, said as he stood in a Christian hospital to which he had made a generous gift: " If Christian people lived up to what they believe, Christianity would sweep the earth." So it would, and so it will, not in animosity to other faiths, but in love for men who deserve the best gifts which their fellows can give them.

IV

WHAT IS THE EFFECT ON MISSIONS OF THE RISING NATIONAL CONSCIOUSNESS AROUND THE WORLD?

A MISSIONARY movement seems logical so long as some nations feel themselves superior to others and these others accept the idea of inferiority. When, however, the receiving nations develop a distinctive national consciousness, they feel differently regarding any organized movement to transfer considerable and influential values from other nations to themselves, especially when those values are intended to supplant their own. Such a movement partakes of the nature of " force," and talk begins about exploitation and imperialism in the field of the spirit. Most national leaders know that nations are changed from within, and many dislike religious or educational or subtle social programmes which tend to alter the character of their people. There might never be serious protest against quiet, single-handed presentation of another religion, but the Christian missionary movement is a strongly organized, well-equipped, self-conscious, aggressive approach to whole areas of the world. Can it continue in presence of this rising tide of national consciousness?   Must it not give way before the logic of nationalism?

I

There are four stages of international relationships.   (*a*) The first stage is a naïve assurance of the superiority of one's own nation.   There the nation stands, long enduring and acceptable; of course others are inferior.   The first envoys of Great Britain to China were counted incapable of appreciating Chinese culture; their gifts were the natural tribute of savage nations to a superior civilization.   (*b*) Under stress of adverse experience this stage is followed by a second—an equally naïve acceptance of the superiority of other nations, together with an over-eagerness to adapt their ways.   These other nations have proved better at some points, such as warfare or commerce; it is supposed that they are better in all ways.   (*c*) This is succeeded by a third stage—a resurgence of nationalism, with contempt for other nations and bitter suspicion of them and their designs.   Since they have proved unfriendly at certain points, they are under suspicion at all points; the patriotic thing is to reduce all contacts as far as possible.   (*d*) This is followed logically by a recovery of normal relations with other nations, seeing their real values, learning from them where lessons are needed, assert-

ing one's own national values where they are
superior.

Nations run this gamut very much as a boy does
in a school. At each stage some things can be done
for the boy or the nation which cannot be done in
other stages.

If it is asked, At what stage are mission lands
today? there is no uniform reply. Probably people
in all lands are in all stages, but nations as a whole
may be found in each of the four. Living men will
recall the progress of China, for example, through
the first two stages—of superiority and inferiority
—and all of us have watched China pass into the
third stage of suspicion of all that is foreign. This
becomes a ground for some Chinese opposition to
Christianity, not because it is bad but because,
being foreign in origin, it must be injurious. In a
small reader supplied to students in China are
these words:

About one hundred years ago, when China opened
her ports to foreign countries, she allowed evangelization by foreigners and the establishment of foreign
Christian schools. . . . Recently the Chinese came to
realize the fact that the missionaries are carrying on a
cultural invasion into China and have been acting as
the instrument of imperialism. Whereupon, an anti-
religious movement was started for the purpose of re-
covering the right of education from foreign hands.

Of course such words are quite aside from the

facts, but no one who knows nationalism can wonder at them. When something is obviously wrong,
everything seems wrong. Multitudes of people in
China would not share this feeling, and such teaching is by no means universal.

Many in India are in this third stage of dislike of all foreign things though here the feeling is much more divided. Some leaders urge
the restoration of everything that is Indian, the
dismissal of all that is British or Western, the
limiting of all religious activities which may lead
to conversion, some adding a wholesale denunciation of any change in personal religious
adherence.

This third stage of rebellion against everything
foreign is a passing one, but it affects missionary
methods and may for a time check some helpful
work. Schools are helpful in making Christ
known; so are hospitals. But Christian schools
require a curriculum in which certain subjects can
almost be taken for granted; if they are denied admission, the duty of maintaining the school is open
to discussion. Ought a Christian mission to maintain schools in which no religious teaching can be
given, voluntary or required? If the law should
forbid the use of even " personal Christian influence " by teachers, should the schools be continued as a Christian enterprise? Hospitals require
doctors and nurses. If the national law or practice
requires registration of foreign doctors and nurses

on conditions which are prohibitive, is a mission obligated to continue its medical work without the especial skill which may come with missionary workers and without the direct Christian influence which such workers bring?

But even if it should be decided that schools and hospitals cannot continue under certain expressions of nationalism, and this is still an open question, that does not affect the major work of missions, for education and medical work are methods, not the work itself. If they cannot be used, then they cannot, but other methods can be continued or introduced. The right of each nation to determine the standards of its own life need not be questioned. Its decisions must be taken as final, even while friends realize that further enlightenment will alter the limitations imposed. This has happened in several marked instances. Indeed, no one who has followed the history of missions will be troubled unduly by hasty restrictions imposed by governments which are just finding themselves and moving through the stage of dislike for all things foreign and unfamiliar. In all nations there are men who never pass beyond that stage. For some in our own nation, if a thing is American, it is good; if it is not American, it is *ipso facto* to be rejected. A land whose people are so widely convinced of one hundred percent Americanism cannot be oversensitive about things that are one hundred percent Chinese or Indian.

There is something strangely familiar about the announcement that in October, 1931, after the Manchurian incident, many Middle School boys in China wore arm-bands whose lettering meant " Eternally never buy Japanese goods." There must be some thousands of Americans under a similar vow regarding goods made in Germany, a vow made in the heat of passion and doubtless quietly abandoned in cooler days. So with the proposal to cut out all English courses in the schools in China; at one time it was strongly urged that German courses should never again be allowed in American schools. While the victim-complex is operating and the under-dog psychology is dominant, anything can be suggested, but the moods pass and reasonable people come into their own again.

And if the restriction runs deeper still and seeks to shut off all external influences, to stop religious efforts of every sort, to hold everything in national hands, as in Mexico at some periods, this also can be endured until a higher enlightenment occurs. Of course in a unified and intertwined world such restrictions are temporary, the expression of a national consciousness which is not yet sure of itself. As time goes on and the national life becomes secure, such restrictions tend to pass away. They are trying and crippling to much of the finest life of the nation while they last, and they shut out much that the nation needs, but there is history back of them, history with which every sincere lover of the land must sympathize. New history must be made, worthier of the day of international unity which has already dawned.

II

Resentment against " superior " nations is based partly on experiences within these nations. At first they were far away and seemed untainted. They brought many excellent and desirable things; it was assumed that all things in them were excellent. Close contact with their actual life creates a very different impression. They are seen to be shot through with evil. Residence in these lands, or even short visits, may lead to disillusionment. The list of wrongs seen and experienced by some Nationals of " mission " lands in "Christian " lands would be too long for insertion here. When an Indian gentleman can travel through America in safety and comfort only by wearing his distinctive turban so that he will not be mistaken for a Negro; when the nations which use force most unsparingly are the Western or " Christian " nations; when it is known that the industrial system has been allowed to dwarf the minds and lives of women and children in these same lands; when the grave inequalities of social position caused by wealth and poverty are realized—when such things become common knowledge, then the offer of a religion which has not corrected these things may be less welcome.

It opens inevitably the question of whether a

religion and the social order with which it is associated can be divorced. Do evils exist in a social order because of or in spite of the prevailing religion? Are the social virtues in spite of or because of the religion to which the people adhere? The question cannot be answered arbitrarily in one way for India and in another way for America. If we blame the religions of India for the evils of the social order, shall we not blame Christianity for the evils of our social order? So argue the people of mission lands.

Here one must discover the attitude which intelligent adherents of a religion take toward social evils and the theory of the religion itself regarding the evils. Does the religion dominate the conditions under which social evils have arisen? Is the religion so generally held that the national life is certainly an expression of its adherents? Has the religion, or have its adherents in its name, a programme of attack on the evils which bids fair to correct them?

III

It must be noted that the correction of evils in the social order is not an act to be done and finished, like cutting down a noxious tree or levelling a difficult hill. This is a process to be begun and continued, not accomplished by radical actions but by reconstruction of life. Most social evils arise from deep-rooted human tendencies, and these are not easily destroyed. The wrong tendencies must be supplanted by wiser ones, safer ones, worthier ones. This requires time and patience. A religion is fairly judged, not by its having achieved the correction of evils, but by its having started the processes of correction and having pushed them forward by a clear and definite and promising programme. If the evils are a constant and accepted challenge to its adherents, then their existence is not a condemnation of the religion.

By such tests as these the Christian faith can be judged. The evils of the social order in which it is working are very real, but they are also very challenging. Nowhere are they more fiercely rebuked and attacked than among Christian adherents, in their pulpits, their books, their programmes. Nothing in the Christian faith can by any stretch of the imagination be called the cause of the evils. Its theory stands dead against them. The process of their correction is steadily advancing.

And this is the plan with all evils. Medical men do not wait to cure all the illness of one land before offering remedies to the rest of the world. Hookworm is a widespread disease for which a preventive and cure have been found in America. But it was never thought that all cases of hookworm must be cured in America before the process of cure was started in other lands. Instead, the Rockefeller Institute reports campaigns now in progress in forty countries. It is complete nowhere; it is begun everywhere. Some day the laboratories will find the cure or preventive for cancer, a dread disease which is almost universal in the world. Immediately the effective cure is learned in one place it will be made available everywhere, without waiting to complete the cure of all cancer cases in any one land.

No thoughtful Christian doubts the power of Christ to correct the evils which concern the whole world, including his own nation. Large groups of believers are now at work in America, Great Britain, and every nominally Christian land, seeking to bring the Gospel of Christ to bear on social evils. It is a long and difficult process, but it is under way. Missionary work is merely starting the same process in other lands. It is not expected that foreigners will complete the process anywhere; that will be the duty of national believers. But foreigners can help to start the process, bringing more and more people into fellowship with God in Christ, which is the initial and central necessity.

This is not a repetition of the familiar saying that Christianity " has never been tried." It is an earnest assertion that it has been widely tried and has accomplished all that is asked of it, and that it is being more and more widely tried with all hope of the best results. Christians believe that Christ can make of America the land it ought to be, and they want to see the process of correction undertaken everywhere else so that the world may become what is in His heart for it.

IV

Here issues the other natural question: How far ought a religion to allow itself to be identified with any one form of political government, so that its messengers can be feared in any sense as representatives of political interests? Christian adherents may properly expect and receive their personal rights of citizenship in any land. They have a right to be Christians wherever they are, and religious liberty is too vital a thing to be lightly surrendered. St. Paul did not consider that becoming a Christian altered his rights as a Roman citizen; he could claim those rights or he could surrender them as occasion might require. But that was for him to choose, not for the Roman Government to determine. An American is just as much a citizen when he goes to other lands to preach Christ as another American is when he goes there to sell sewing machines or oil. Demanding that he drop his citizenship when he goes out on the errand of religion makes an entirely wrong impression regarding religion. It does not denationalize any man to become a Christian. This is exactly what some uninformed Chinese and Africans fear, and if they found that Americans or Britons actually do lose their citizenship because of their religion, their fears would be confirmed. Christianity ought to make better and firmer Chinese, Americans, Africans, each in his own relationship.

Yet any one can see the value of holding this right flexibly. Missionaries do not ask military protection. No Protestant Board of Missions would ask on its own account any indemnity for the life of a missionary. His life is a gift which has no price. Sometimes individuals or surviving families make their independent claim for indemnity when life is lost, but while this is within their rights, it has seemed to Boards an unwise use of the right. Sometimes, also, quite apart from missionary desire, governments have made adverse experiences of missionaries the ground for reprisals, but for this the missionary enterprise is unjustly blamed. The famous instance wherein two German missionaries were killed in a province in China, which was made the occasion for demanding a large commercial concession, is a case in point. This was never desired by the missionary society whose missionaries were killed, and that society received no benefit from it, but rather loss, since it developed exactly the spirit which is most fatal to mission work.

The issue is discussed in *The Indian Social Reformer,* November 28, 1931. A political official had insisted that missionaries necessarily have " special political privileges as Europeans in India," and that the Round Table Conference should take this into account. No missionary supported

this contention.   Rev. William Paton, Secretary of
the International Missionary Council, was undis-
puted when he replied:

> I should frankly deplore it as a spiritual disaster if
> missionary rights were urged by British champions at
> the Round Table Conference along with the right of
> freedom to foreign traders. . . . The future of the mis-
> sionary enterprise lies within the future of the Indian
> Church, and the real ground on which the full freedom
> of the enterprise should be based is in the fact that it
> is an integral part of the whole Christian life of India.

In similar terms ten representative missionaries
from various missions wrote:

> Speaking for ourselves and expressing the mind, as
> we believe, of most of our colleagues in India, we wish
> to make it clear that we missionaries desire no special
> political privileges as Europeans in India.

The *Reformer* welcomes this as expressing the
missionary sentiment throughout the land.

Property indemnities have been differently esti-
mated by different missionary agencies.   One chief
trouble is that the people who have to pay the indemnities are virtually never the ones who did the
damage.   A mob burns a hospital or a school, often
a mob from a distance, but the citizens of the place
have generally to pay the indemnities.   When it is
evident that the restoration of the property will
not be an undue burden and that its value to the
community will be clear and unquestioned, some

Boards have encouraged or accepted indemnity and restoration. It is a moot question. But any suggestion that missionaries are at their posts under the powerful protection of alien governments is utterly foolish. It has never been true; it is not now true.

The Christian faith requires no single form of government. It has worked under democracy, monarchy, aristocracy, and any form that has arisen; it is not yet proved that it cannot work under a sane and intelligent communism. It does not ask the destruction of any governmental system in itself. An oppressive government is unsuited to it. A government that disregards personality and hinders freedom of initiative will not be suited to its genius. But it identifies itself with no system of political agencies; it is an enemy of none. Its adherents seek to render to the civil powers the duties which they may properly require, while rendering to God the duties which belong to Him.

Nothing in current conditions changes any of this. The nerve of missions is nowhere cut by a nationalism which continues to count itself part of a world and not isolated from it. There is an ineffective internationalism as there is a narrow nationalism, but between true internationalism and true nationalism there is no collision. The Christian enterprise frankly takes its place as the aid of both.

V

There still remains the question of the duty of a
missionary regarding patriotic movements in the
country where he works. No difficulty arises so
long as the national life is quiet and undisturbed.
This is no longer true of most nations. Such definite " sides " are formed that it is difficult for a
missionary to hold the regard of the Nationals if
he refuses to take one of these " sides." Yet often
the people themselves are deeply divided and in
some cases, as in India, the difficulty involves two
National groups. Missionaries are often criticized
for their hesitation at this point. Those who do
not hesitate are often as severely criticized.

Most Mission Boards and missionary groups
take the position that in a real sense missionaries
are guests in the lands where they work. They
retain their citizenship in the sending countries,
though they intend to live in the country of their
work. The prevailing practice is to maintain the
same balance of public action which marks a
thoughtful minister in a church in America during
a violent presidential campaign. No one suspects
for a moment that he has not his own convictions
and no one objects to his expressing them in wise
ways. But no minister at such a time would organize his church work nor regulate his pulpit
utterances so that he was committed to one side or
the other of the political issue. This is always
difficult for earnest men. It is difficult for mis-

sionaries, but there seems no escape from the necessity of maintaining an honest balance both of judgment and of expression at such a time. It must be expected that there will be lack of appreciation of this effort, and strong Nationalists on one " side " or another will discount missionaries who do not stand with them. They have to remember, however, that if the missionary stands with one group, he forfeits his standing with another, and he is not there to take part in the regulating of the political life of the nation. If the only way to carry on mission work is to choose " sides " in an internal controversy, then missionary work would be greatly hampered. If, on the other hand, it is possible to carry on the work with a sincere concern for the total interests of the country and of its people, then all that is necessary is sagacity, good judgment, and a good spirit on the part of the missionary.

There is, thus, no necessary antagonism between the rising spirit of nationalism and the Christian movement. In its earlier, cruder, more anxious forms, when all things foreign are opposed, Christianity will have to bear the marks of its foreign origin and of the alien citizenship of its first messengers. But this is a passing stage, and missionaries are not involved in the internal struggle for this as the form of government. They are always on the errand of the spirit, messengers of goodwill between God and man and among all men.

ARE PREVAILING MISSIONARY METHODS SUITED TO THE PRESENT CON- DITION OF THE WORLD?

MISSIONARY methods must obviously vary with the world which they are meant to serve. However determined the workers may be, their methods must be flexible enough to get the work done. Is this actually oc- curring? Have missionaries and their sustaining Boards been sufficiently sensitive to the changes in world conditions? Has not the work become static and rigid, following the same old round per- sistently but unsuccessfully?

I

Since there are a great many missionaries in a great many places with a great many different ideas of what they are trying to accomplish, it is certain that there are rigid, unbending, dogmatic workers with methods unsuited to the task. Some of them will be doggedly opposed to any effort to accom- modate their work to changed conditions, counting it a wicked compromise. Some of them have be- come firmly settled in their ways and will not change. Some have swung so far away from familiar methods that their colleagues have reacted strongly against their new ideas. This merely means that missionaries have come out of home churches and bear the characteristics of those churches. It will hardly be claimed that all churches in Christendom have caught step with their times as adequately as they might have done, and it is not surprising if their representatives in other lands are equally rigid. But, as many churches in the home lands seriously try to serve in ways suited to their communities, so it may be expected that their representatives in other lands will seek to fit into their new homes.

II

Everything turns, however, on what one counts the purpose of the Christian religion. Suppose it did everything it is meant to do, what would that be? Clearly, one's programme of missionary work will be laid out according to the answer to that question.

A missionary may ask either or both of two questions: What should be the programme of the Gospel? and, What are the needs of the people whom I seek to serve? There may be some things of Christian concern which are being supplied by other agencies. They may then be omitted from the missionary programme. On the other hand, missionaries may welcome many changes in social

or political life which they do not feel it their duty
to seek as part of their work. For example: the
economic level of a people should be lifted; they
should have better homes; they should be better
protected against cold and disease. Good men welcome every improvement in this regard. But they
differ in deciding whether this is the business of
missions. Some say the missionaries do not go out
to change social systems but rather to change the
spiritual relationships of men to God and each
other, in assurance that this will sooner or later
take care of the other needs. Are such things in
the missionary programme? If so, it will require
a set of methods which can be entirely omitted if
they are not involved in missionary work. Workers cannot be judged upon their methods until one
knows what they are trying to do, what they think
they ought to do.

(*a*) Home critics of missionaries sometimes
blame them for using other than direct soul-seeking
methods, discounting hospitals and schools and
similar items. They think these methods divert
energy from more important work. The critics
ought to realize that these agencies are sharply
criticized on the field for their too effective propa-
ganda value. In India both Mr. Gandhi and Mr.
Natarajan, editor of the *Indian Social Reformer,*
protest earnestly against hospital service as a missionary method. They think that no one should
seek to commend his religion to those whom he

helps in this way. When a convert told Mr. Gandhi of his joy in his new-found Christian faith, Mr. Gandhi was sincerely pleased, but when the convert asked him whether he should not tell other people, Mr. Gandhi could not answer. The suggestion collided with his teaching of the impropriety of seeking to bring another to one's own faith. Mr. Natarajan feels that missionaries should live austerely like the " holy men " of India, and thus commend their faith on its own merits.

But suppose it is of the essence of a religion to help the sick and afflicted, to share with others the riches of one's belief, to avoid the lower limits of living and to move on higher levels better suited to human rights and duties—then are the methods improper which illustrate this? What shall a missionary physician do when he is serving the sick? Is he not there solely because his religion has sent him there, and is not his hospital a natural and proper method of commending his religion? And what if living like an Indian " holy man " is a sheer infraction of the main principles of the Christian faith? What if the purpose of the faith is to open wider and richer doors into living? Then does not a missionary commend his faith best by methods that reveal this richer life?

(b) A further complication lies in the fact that methods cannot be adapted merely to what men may want; they must take into account also what men ought to want. If it is objected that a certain

group are happier without Christ or the Christian
religion, the question still remains whether they
ought to be. " Better be a man dissatisfied than a
brute satisfied "—is that valid?   Men may be happy
on such low levels that their manhood is endan-
gered.   Their very happiness and contentment will
be their peril.   The first duty of a friend may be
to cause dissatisfaction and unhappiness.   It is true
in the field of music and art and manners; why
not also in the field of religion and standards of
conduct?

The principle holds widely.   Our fathers did not
complain about the way they lighted their houses;
they were as well satisfied as the people of interior
China may be with their way.   But that way of
lighting a house has its serious losses which can be
made good by better ways, ways of which they
would never have heard if no one had disturbed
their satisfaction.   The religious practices of some
peoples are satisfactory to many of them, but they
ought not to be satisfactory if religion is valid at
all.   If Jesus is right in any sense it cannot be well
for men to think of God as some of them do think
of Him.   Yet if a man is wedded to his poor idea
of God, it may be painful to have it pointed out
that it is poor and unworthy.   In the long run, of
course, the higher idea is the idea of greater happiness; it is something a man direfully needs.   But
he may not know it.   Methods of missionary work
must be found which do lead to higher and worthier

living, thinking, conduct, relationship, for this is what men need and what Christ wants, whether at the first they want it themselves or not.

(c) Suppose it is agreed that the Christian religion is meant to supply human needs; it would still be possible to scale these needs and to argue that some of them are so much more vital than others that the less vital could be passed by. If a building were burning and a child were to be rescued, it would be sheer folly to give time and attention to an extra dish of food that might be on the table in his room or to laying straight a rug on the floor. These are desirable things in their time and place, but they shrink into nothing in presence of really critical needs. So many missionary agencies feel.

Men need to be set right with God; they are terribly wrong with Him. In presence of that need everything else seems futile and unimportant. Keeping a missionary at one place to teach schoolboys to play games or to show mothers a better way of bathing their babies seems poor economy when there are vast areas where the first saving word of the Gospel has never been spoken—so many missionary agencies, but not many missionaries, feel. Establishing schools which eat up missionary personnel for the teaching of arithmetic and writing, with the Bible on the side, seems remote from the main task. All decent men rejoice in the results if they can be brought about without neglect of far greater things; but some gravely question whether this can be done.

Or, one may become tremendously impressed with and concerned for the intelligence of a people. Why present any religion to people who are left untrained? How can there be a Christian Church without trained leaders? Mr. H. G. Wells says history is a race between education and catastrophy. Missionaries who feel this about the lands where they work will go strong on schools and education. Or, the need may be economic. How can an impoverished people, living below a decent level, realize the truth of such a faith as Christianity? Hence a primary duty would be to introduce better economic conditions and methods, establish agricultural and industrial agencies and send out missionaries trained for the work.

Among most missionaries such distinctions are less real than this wording suggests. They see the need for all these things, for they think of the Gospel as intended to supply the whole round of human need; even in its first stages they want it to face the total task. In the nature of the case, they cannot attempt everything, but they can leave the way open for each new method when the possibility of effective use of it develops. The full Christian programme surely includes all these lines of service; its missionary aspect need not attempt all of them at the same time. Still, it is fair to urge that it shall be so laid out that as the full Christian programme develops there will be no wrench of conviction among the national believers. They ought to know from the first that this will come before long.

Meanwhile, it continues to be a danger of missionary effort that workers will centralize on some one phase of it to the entire exclusion of other phases—will become institutionalized to such an extent that no spiritual expansion occurs, or will become so devoted to expansion that new believers are left untrained in the faith which they have received.

III

There seems no good reason for abandoning any of the seven familiar and prevailing missionary methods: evangelistic, educational, medical, literary, philanthropic, industrial, social. At one point or another they touch all individual human needs, and when they are kept in wise balance they present the full programme of the Gospel and start the new believers on their way with right guidance.

New developments may be expected in each of them with the changing times. For example, it has now become possible to send to mission lands English-speaking lecturers who can reinforce the more local missionary teaching. The first lecturer to attempt this service, as far back as 1881, was the well-known Boston Monday lecturer, Joseph Cook. Several Missions now call for English-speaking evangelists who may come to re-arouse the zeal of national ministers and other workers. Christian scientists and philosophers can now render a large service by courses of lectures in their own language in many lands. Such service could not have been effectively rendered until knowledge of the English language became fairly common.

In most lands the first Christian appeal was to the uncultured and ignorant. Only they were open to the Gospel. The methods were adapted to them, sometimes it was almost assumed that the appeal could be to no others in the land. The Christian faith had its historical beginning on this same level. One recalls the well-known sneer of Celsus when he pretends to speak for the early Christians:

Let no educated man enter, no wise man, no prudent man, for such things we deem evil; but whoever is ignorant, whoever is unintelligent, whoever is uneducated, whoever is simple, let him come and be welcome.

This sounds very foolish to us, but it sounds also like Paul's word in I Corinthians 1:26-29. Paul knew it would seem so to the people of Corinth, second only to Athens in intellectual culture. "Not many wise,"—not many, but some. They always emerge early, as Paul himself did, but the faith must continue to provide for the simple and uncultured as well.

In some places missionary methods have doubtless remained on this lower level and have not taken sufficient account of the presence of the cultured and intelligent classes in society. In that case the correction lies to hand. It will be a change in accent and approach rather than in substance. Christianity may start on the lower levels; it never stays there. Its danger is that it may utterly forsake those levels. Meanwhile, it must make such changes as its changed appeal requires. It may be fairly criticized if it fails to do so.

Increased literacy among common people makes increased literary effort logical and resultful. On the other hand, the development of adequate systems of medical education, as in Japan, lessens the accent on this great arm of service in some lands, though it must still be used in large areas of the missionary enterprise. The growth of national churches has made it necessary to give larger attention to the training of leaders and other workers under the guidance of these churches. This has also underscored the value of industrial methods in order to make possible a self-supporting and self-propagating church. Indeed, no one who knows the missionary force in any wide field can suppose that its methods are standardized everywhere. It would be difficult to name any method of commending Christ to men which some missionary is not now using or has not used and abandoned as ineffective. Very novel methods have the same difficulty in missions as elsewhere, but some workers are always trying them.

IV

Probably critics of missions think most frequently of the change of accent around the world on the true service of religion. The heavy accent was once on religion as fitting men for eternal destiny. Its temporal service was never entirely overlooked, but it was made secondary and was often slightly regarded in Christian programmes. In all lands the accent has changed during recent years. Eternal destiny enters far less into the thought of Christian workers everywhere than it did formerly. What was once secondary has become, for many of them, primary. Religion is meant, they feel, for the life that now is, to change present conditions, to make this world the world it ought to be in the purpose of God and to fit men for living in it in right relations with each other. So great has been the change that large numbers of workers have almost lost the earlier and major accent. They say so much about time that they forget eternity, so much about man that they say little about God, so much about ethics that they omit salvation.

Now, if critics feel that this change has cut the nerve of missions and that present methods are out of date when they do not take full account of it, the issue may become a very real one. No missionary activity can be carried on for long or with full power on the narrower, this-worldly, temporal, ethical basis alone. There are no instances of success in such a programme. There are, on the other hand, some instances of remarkably helpful programmes that moved without reference to these temporal elements. The instances do not prove the wisdom of the programme, but the entire lack of instances of the other sort would suggest the probable defect of the idea. There has been plenty of time for somebody to attempt the plan of making a missionary programme which omits eternity and the spiritual needs of men, but it has never been carried on long enough to reveal any lasting vitality. The only hope for it seems to be to attach it in some way to the other type of work.

The danger of secularizing missionary schools and transferring what was meant to be a method of Christian progress into a mere training of the mind, important as that may be, has troubled missionary workers for some time. With a real love for education and an unshaken belief in its proper ministry to humanity, it remains true that its purely secular aspects are not the major concern of missionary efforts. Governments are often better able to maintain such schools than private individuals or foreign funds. Yet some governments realize the need for something further, and this further thing is the main task of the Church. The Japanese Minister for Education, in 1931, addressed a communication to Christian missionaries which he authorized them to publish. In it he said:

Hitherto the policy of our ministry has been too

materialistic, and this has led to the regrettable result
of a decline in public and private morality, a revival of
communism, and even in the last few years of a pro-
nounced anarchistic spirit. We must from now onward
spiritualize our educational system. For this purpose,
the co-operation of religious educational institutions
seems to us absolutely necessary, and we consequently
make an urgent appeal for your help.

Any missionary programme which does not take
account of this increased accent upon the service
of religion for life here and now is defective. The
only danger is that it may swing so far over that
it loses its only vitalizing energy. If man is not
treated as an immortal being, with eternal desti-
nies, then a vital part of the truth is omitted, for
man is that kind of a being according to any thor-
ough Christian consideration. Life here is of
greater importance because it leads on to a life in
which character and relationship to God are fundamental. Missionaries must not be asked to forget
that fact nor to shape their methods as though it
were not so.

v

Another question arises out of the rapid growth
of national churches. Are not missionary methods
based too much on an earlier condition, when missionaries were pioneers or paternal, directing new
believers, maintaining control of all movements and
institutions, determining all courses of advance,

supervising everything? There was such a time, but in most lands it has passed. In so far as missionary methods continue on the old basis in those lands, they are belated. The old phrase of working " for " the Chinese, or Japanese, or Siamese, has given way to the phrase of working " with " them. Some missionaries feel that the movement is going too rapidly and that the national church is really not ready to carry the responsibility of the Christian enterprise. Others think the national believers are ready for it if they can be really released from their long experience of being managed. Instances of belated paternalism can be found; some of them may easily become notable in the eyes of critics of the enterprise. But the swing of the movement undoubtedly does take account of this interesting and desirable fact of growing consciousness and ability in the national churches. From the very beginning it has been realized that just this condition would arise. It has been prayed for and worked for. But its coming in many places has been more rapid than was expected and the call to a new stage of Christian progress has come to many who are accustomed to earlier conditions.

The transition is not easy to make, but probably it is being generally made as gracefully and effectively as could be expected. More and more the control is passing to the hands where it belongs.

But any suggestion that missionary work may, on that account, be completed or be nearing com-

pletion, is based on sheer ignorance of the actual
facts on mission fields.   There are lands where no
such church has yet developed in any remote sense;
in no land has it yet developed so that missionary
aid can be wisely withdrawn and missionary counsel be abandoned.   No sagacious national leaders
even suggest such a thing.   With one voice they
call for reinforcements and a continuance of missionary aid in their work.   They do uniformly desire that new workers shall be co-operative rather
than dominating, but this is no news to missionary
agencies.   In most lands the era of missionary
domination has long passed.   Inevitable and proper
at the first, it would be eminently improper now.
Wherever missionaries retain even a semblance of
it, criticism is sure to be aroused, but it is a passing
condition.

VI

A different phase of the problem introduced by
the rise of the national churches is that of the suitable and Christian relation between missionaries
and national workers on the financial side.   How
far should foreign money be used in the support
of national workers and on what scale should any
recompense be adjusted?   This is the knottiest
single problem in this particular field.   Missionary
salaries are in no sense a recompense for the work
done; they are intended merely to provide a rea-
sonably comfortable living in the place where the

work is done. Shall the national church, instead, hope to compete with remunerative occupations in securing and holding its workers? The churches in Christendom do not try to do so. Church salaries are generally on a much lower scale than men of similar calibre receive in secular business. The Church on the field finds it cannot compete with teaching and business in its salary scale. So it loses some of its best workers. Is the escape found in putting national workers more nearly on the missionary (or foreign) scale? How far is it wise to raise Christian workers above the economic level of their people and to remove their uncertainties of support by the use of assured foreign money? It is certain that this would involve a much longer period of dependency than any one hopes for, because it scales the financial demands of the Church far above its resources for years to come. Missionaries are on this scale, not because for them it is high; on the contrary, it is often too low to be entirely safe. They have family obligations also which they do not share with their national brethren, the education of their children, the provision for old age, the refreshment of mind and spirit required because they come out of another form of life at a later age than their national colleagues. Some missionary homes are more pretentious than they ought to be; some missionaries live much too far from their national colleagues, losing helpfulness by it; some others live unsuitably on a lower level, teaching no helpful lessons about home or personal life. Careful thinking will reveal reasons for the scale ordinarily adopted for missionary living, with admission here and there of unwise application of the scale up or down.

But when this is said, the question remains about the use of foreign money in payment of salaries of national workers. Can the missionary enterprise be carried on successfully on the basis of mere money gifts? If the missionaries were withdrawn and the money for their present support were handed to the national church, supporting a larger number of national workers, would this be a blessing? Most observers think that it would not be a blessing and that the churches at home would not carry the burden if it did not involve gifts of life as well as money.

The case can be rested on the actual value to the national churches of this form of aid. A number of fields already show the weakening effect of too long dependence on foreign finances. The self-respect of workers is lowered, the programme of the national church is scaled beyond the support of its own people, cutting the nerve of their responsibility, Christianity continues to appear to the surrounding observers as an outside, foreign affair. It is difficult to find instances where the ultimate results have been good. In pioneer work it is often necessary for missionary money to support workers, there being no other possible provision for them. But with the rising of the Church, the case changes and it is well for workers to take their places among their own fellows as workers in the West have to do, even though their friends receive larger recompense for their service than they can hope to receive. Hardly a missionary can be found whose college classmates are not receiving far ampler salaries and far richer provision for living than their missionary friends. It will be so in all mission lands among the young believers.

The problem is not easily solved and room must be made for many exceptions to any fixed rule. But the rise of the national churches does not undo the work of missionaries nor lessen the necessity for its continuance, now as colleagues in the work where once they were the leaders and directors. Each needs to stand on his own feet in financial support, the missionary supported by the sending church, the national worker by his own church. From this will come the truly indigenous, self-governing, self-supporting Church.

VII

One further danger in this field of methods is that an assumption of superiority in the culture of sending lands may prevent the wise use of high and worthy elements in the cultures of receiving lands. A notable Commission on Higher Christian Education in India, reporting to the Boards in 1931, vividly voiced this danger as follows:

The Christian colleges as they stand [in India] are
not only teachers of Christianity; they are teachers of
characteristic British and American culture. We believe that both Britain and America have much to give
to modern India, but only on condition that modern
India is free to take from Britain and America what
she needs and use it for her own purposes. She is not
likely to submit to cultural domination.

Complaints of this sort come from other lands—
the feeling that too little thought is given to the
keeping of elements in the native life and thought
which are worthy and suitable to the Christian
faith. It is a natural continuance of the time when
little had been learned about the higher life and
thought of other lands and it constitutes in itself
a serious problem of adjustment of methods. This
adjustment is being made in many institutions and
in many lands in the form of Church organization
and worship. In many places it still needs to be
made. The Christian faith has a great capacity for
absorption of the good which it meets and the
transformation of it to forms suited to the life of
the people. It permits no one of its groups to
dominate another culturally beyond the good of
both. Whenever this is done, the work deserves
criticism, but missionaries are increasingly alive to
the need for preserving the values which mark the
new habitat of the Christian faith.

VI

WHAT IS THE PRESENT CONDITION OF THE WORK?—SURVEYED BY COUNTRIES

DOES the work of missions show anywhere signs of completion? Does it suggest failure? If we survey the actual work today are we reassured or are we disturbed? Are stories of failure authentic, and could they account for the inactivity of the missionary organ in the Church body?

I

No statement about missions could be more temporary and less satisfactory than one which tries to answer this question. In so large an enterprise it should be clear that no one thing is true everywhere. Each illustration of progress can be matched by another which indicates that wheels drag. In 1832, one hundred years ago, Dr. Samuel F. Smith wrote the missionary hymn beginning, " The morning light is breaking," in which occur these lines:

> Each breeze that sweeps the ocean
>   Brings tidings from afar
> Or nations in commotion
>   Prepared for Zion's war.

In the same year, Thomas Hastings wrote, " Hail to the brightness of Zion's glad morning," in which he declared that:

> Fall'n are the engines of war and commotion,
>   Shouts of salvation are rending the sky.

Both of these hymns are worthy expressions of Christian assurance, and both of them can be confirmed by instances here and there.   But does not everyone know that many breezes that sweep the ocean bring quite different tidings from afar, and is it not clear that the engines of war and commotion have not fallen even yet?   This is a large world, and almost anything is true of some place in it.

Meanwhile, we must remember that all the world was once a missionary field.   Great Britain, France, Europe, America have all been the scene of vast missionary labours.   If inquiry had been made at the beginning about any one of them, many sagacious observers would have discouraged effort.   Only the adventurous believed in it.   Yet the work could not possibly be counted a failure though it took years of struggle and sacrifice.   The Christian work is nowhere fully done in these lands, but the " missionary " part of it is over. There is the same reason for expecting that it will some day be done in those parts of the world which are now " missionary " territory.   Has " missionary " work ever succeeded?   Yes, if success means the establishing of the Christian faith in a land so that its own people carry the work forward. Every " Christian " land in the world is an instance of such success. The Christian faith has always been introduced from outside the land itself. It has never sprung up spontaneously from the soil of the popular mind. What is happening now in " missionary " lands is just what happened in all present " Christian " lands.

In any missionary survey of the present world we must avoid the error of making any one instance or any one range of facts normal for the whole. An outbreak occurs in one part of China in which missionaries are counted part of the " foreign aggression." Immediately, one type of missionary critic sees China in rebellion and calls on missionaries everywhere to abandon all connection with their home governments and to " nationalize their work," in order to succeed. The fact may easily be that most of China has no thought of such need, partly because most missionaries have not claimed governmental connection and partly because the work is already largely nationalized. Or, a missionary in India becomes prominent for action unwelcome to the ruling powers, and a call is sounded for release of missionaries from the limiting condition, whereas the condition may not prevail and most missionaries do not ask the right to determine the internal issues of the Empire.

On the other hand, a vigorous national church emerges in one section, taking over large direction of the work and some measure of its support. Enthusiastic observers cite it as a normal condition and demand that the same thing be immediately developed in other places, though their people may be utterly unfitted for it. It is mere common-sense to measure each field and condition by itself rather than by others radically different. Simple as that dictate seems, it is exceedingly difficult in practice.

II

It may be helpful for some readers to look over a list of the major " mission lands " with a brief word regarding the task of the Christian faith in each land. The list can have no final value, but may be enlarged and safeguarded by wider study.

1. AFRICA. This is really a collection of many fields with widely varied conditions. In some parts of the interior there are many who can still be counted " heathen," " pagans," " savages,"—words which cannot be applied to all non-Christians but need not be abandoned where they still apply. The " religion " of these groups includes a large variety of animistic paganism, sometimes of a highly self-conscious type. In the north, especially in Egypt and Abyssinia, are several early forms of Christianity, some of which greatly need reformation.

Egypt is also the site of the largest educational work of Islam or Mohammedanism. There is a strong influence of Islam issuing from this centre and showing itself in a wide band of Moslems about midway across the Continent. This large group has been developed chiefly by Moslem merchants who have carried their religious practices with them. Farther south, approaching the Cape, the Dutch and British influence has developed a large Christian population which tends to move into the interior both by migration and by missions. There is now growing in Africa a national consciousness which may produce a much closer unity than has ever been known. Perhaps nowhere in the world are interracial issues more sharp than in the southern part. Very little of the land is under African control; most of it is divided among European nations in the form either of colonies or of mandates. Meantime, most of the Continent has been surveyed and included in some missionary project, though most of these projects are yet inadequate to the needs. Many large institutions have developed and native leadership is emerging in most sections. Africa continues to be a vast missionary field with a bewildering variety of languages and racial customs still to be studied and mastered.

2. AFGHANISTAN. This is a country of about 8,000,000 people, strongly Moslem, of sects that

are so extreme that many Moslems do not recognize them. It is entirely closed to all Christian work and no missionaries of any sort are found in the country. The ruler made a visit to Europe in 1928 and announced large plans for modernizing the people and their customs, but they were widely repudiated by the native leaders. A small group of Christians was permitted to enter the land on a brief visit in 1929, merely to do medical work without preaching. It seems to have been found, however, that this work raised too many religious questions and a later request for a repetition of the visit was refused. Mission stations near the borders of Afghanistan, in other lands, are under much suspicion and their movements are carefully watched lest they attempt missionary work across the border. Thus far it is an untouched missionary territory.

3. ARABIA. This is the historic land and the present stronghold of Islam, the site of Mecca and Medina, which non-Moslems can visit only at their peril. The people are largely nomads, fanatical and bigoted, living in scattered settlements in primitive fashion, with several larger centres of permanent population. Mission work is done at a number of points and medical work has been especially welcomed. Nothing in the nature of a native church exists and there are few professing Christians. The incursion of modern life is observed

with some anxiety by conservative Moslems, many of the pilgrims to Mecca now coming in motor-cars from the borders. A " filling station " is reported close by the Kaaba, the most sacred edifice in Arabia! Aggressive Christian work must be done with great caution in the land.

4. CHINA. In many senses this continues to be the greatest missionary field in the world, and most missionary agencies are represented in it at some point or points. In a population of more than four hundred millions there are probably not more than five million professing Christians, but these are far more influential in the national life than their numbers would suggest. The President of the Republic is (1932) a Christian, as are several members of his Cabinet. The prevailing system of faith is Confucianism, an indigenous system, whose religious quality is much disputed by Chinese themselves, many of whom count it an ethical system suited to any religion one may choose to follow. Certainly it is held by many in connection with Buddhism, which was imported into China from India. There is a considerable population of Moslems. Some of the leaders of thought are frankly atheistic. The religious practices of the interior are largely the residuum of generations of family and community practices, often followed with no understanding of their purpose or meaning. Taoism is widely prevalent, its history also being en-

tirely Chinese; it is also compatible with other religions and it is not uncommon to find a Chinese who counts himself a Confucianist, a Taoist and a Buddhist at the same time. One of the questions often raised about the Christian faith in China is whether it may not be properly added to those already held. The Roman Catholic missionaries have blurred the line at this point considerably and have seemed to sacrifice some of the central Christian demands. Protestants have not inclined to reject the ethical system of Confucius where this does not cross the track of religion in either its denial of God or its estimate of the worth of human personality. There is little opposition to Christianity itself, but it often meets opposition because of its foreign connection. When anti-foreign and anti-religious forces combine, the way of Christian believers is often difficult. There is a growing national church with increasing unity, taking over much of responsibility at certain points. Missionaries work " with " the Chinese at most points rather than " for " them.

5. INDIA. Next to China, this is the major mission field of the world, second in population among mission lands. The fact that it is part of the British Empire has accented the responsibility of the missionary agencies of Great Britain. India has therefore fewer workers from other lands, though American work is very common. The presence of

large numbers of Christian believers from Great Britain in governmental and commercial service is generally favourable, though the natural inference that all British residents are Christians produces much confusion among the natives.

(*a*) The prevailing religion is Hinduism, which dates from before recorded history and takes multitudinous forms, so that no one can safely say just when a practice or a community is Hindu or when it is not. Popular Hinduism is polytheistic, uses caste distinctions, and many of its practices seem to observers highly superstitious. (*b*) About one-fourth of the population is Moslem, though this is an imported faith, making the introduction of any other religion perfectly logical. Between Moslems and Hindus there is an unfortunate and aggressive rivalry and opposition which affects all plans for national betterment and progress. (*c*) Buddhism originated in India as a reform movement against Brahmin Hinduism, but it is much stronger elsewhere than here. The Buddhist population is comparatively small. (*d*) Many smaller religious groups exist—Parsees, Sikhs, reform movements such as the Arya Somaj, the Brahmo Somaj, Seva Sedan. (*e*) The Christian groups are numerous, totalling probably six million in a population of over three hundred millions. Strong efforts are made to bring the groups into closer unity, and several " united " churches have been formed. All forms of missionary work are carried on. A very early Christian group, supposed to have been started by the Apostle Thomas in the first century, is found on the West Coast south of Bombay. There is little opposition to Christianity, though complete independence from the British Empire might lead to opposition to it as part of the foreign influence. American missionaries would probably feel the opposition less than the British, however, for the above reasons. There is a vast field here still for missionaries of the right spirit and adequate equipment.

6. INDO-CHINA. This little-known section of Southeastern Asia, under the control of France, has been largely closed to Protestant missionary work until recently. It has now become possible to undertake more aggressive work. The religion is chiefly Buddhist, where the original animism or spirit-worship has been altered. Moslem influence appears also, coming up from the Malayan Islands and peninsula. The population is about twenty millions. Naturally, however, Catholic workers have been permitted to preach here as in all French possessions, and there are several Catholic mission stations. Protestant missionaries have never been cordially welcomed, though their work would now be possible. Of course there is no Protestant group ready to take responsibility for carrying on Christian evangelization. It is an open missionary field not yet occupied. Some Christian influences have

come into it from China and from Siam through travellers and migration of Christians.

7. IRAK (MESOPOTAMIA). This is Moslem territory, feeling the modification of Moslem practices but still strongly set toward Islam. Since the War it has been a French mandate, but is now becoming independent with articles of agreement which guarantee religious liberty both of instruction and of profession. There is no self-conscious Christian Church here; it is a wide and promising missionary field.

8. JAPAN. Still one of the major missionary fields partly in itself and partly in its possession of Formosa, which is one of the remaining sections properly spoken of as containing " heathen " or " pagans " in the interior. This description has long passed in Japan proper, where literacy has become virtually universal after an amazing advance during three generations. (a) Shinto is the indigenous religion, though it is counted rather a national and patriotic cult than a complete religious faith. Certain of its earlier practices, then counted religious, are now required of students and public officials as purely patriotic. (b) The prevailing religion is Buddhism, imported from India as a foreign faith but now adapted to Japanese life. (c) The Christian Church is entirely self-governing, though some Western divisions continue in

spite of many efforts at fuller " union." The number of enrolled Christian believers (church members) is still comparatively small, but it includes some of the most aggressive people of the land. The leadership of Christian work is almost entirely in Japanese hands, though it will be necessary for some time to send missionaries to reinforce their efforts, particularly in large areas not yet evangelized. Financial support is still needed and welcomed, as are missionaries in many lines. Little medical missionary work is needed because of local advance in modern medicine. Educational work is needed for the sake of Church leadership and as a means of " leavening society " with the Christian Gospel. The majority of the population are far from an intelligent understanding of the Christian faith. Japanese leaders expect and desire missionaries to be sent for further service.

9. KOREA, officially CHOSEN. This is a dependency of Japan but for missionary history can be considered separately. The prevailing religion was spiritism or animism, affected naturally by the proximity of Buddhism in Japan and Confucianism in China. The first movements of modern missions occurred during the eighties of the last century and the response to Christian appeal has been very remarkable. There are about half a million believers in a population of eighteen millions. The churches are self-directing and largely self-

propagating; they are increasingly self-supporting, though many of the institutions of modern Christianity are too heavy a burden to be independently borne as yet. The Japanese Government is now laying such restrictions on medical practice that such work may decrease, but there is no likelihood of the ending of educational or evangelistic work for a long time. It is still one of the most hopeful and resultful missionary fields.

10. LATIN AMERICA. This general term covers a wide variety of missionary conditions, from Mexico, through Central America, to the end of the South American Continent. It must not be assumed that it is a homogeneous country. In South America alone there are seventy-five languages properly considered independent of any other linguistic stock in any other part of the world. Added languages are found in Central America and Mexico. Any approach to the present generation must be through their languages, many of which are not yet reduced to writing. It is generally thought of as a Roman Catholic section, but there is a large population of Indians in the interior of all the countries who are pagan and superstitious and have not been reached by Roman Catholic influences. Next to them is a wide fringe of people who have felt some of the Christian impulses and have become " baptized pagans," as a Roman Catholic writer once described them. Latin Amer-

ican Catholicism has never felt the effect of a
Reformation and the counter-reformation which
that movement provoked. It cannot, therefore, be
measured by the American type of Catholicism.
It is more superstitious, less intelligent, much more
formal and less spiritual. If it seems necessary to
make Christ known where He is not known, it would
seem mere loyalty to make Him known where He
is misrepresented and misunderstood and obscured
by practices which are contrary to His spirit.

Protestant work is done in all the nineteen republics of Latin America and most of the agencies
at work are included in the Committee for Co-
operation in Latin America, which attempts to
unify the work and to prevent overlapping of
effort. The work does not attempt to unsettle the
Roman Catholic population; there is much more
than Protestants can do in caring for the already
unsettled and estranged population. It will be a
missionary field calling for evangelism and education for years to come. Because of Roman Catholic history, governmental restrictions are addressed
against all evangelical religions in many of the
republics, but these will pass as the political power
of that Church ceases and full religious liberty may
be expected as in all enlightened countries.

11. MALAYASIA, INCLUDING THE PENINSULA
AND THE SOUTH SEA ISLANDS. This is one of the
most interesting and open missionary fields of the

world. The prevailing religion is Mohammedanism, but with a strong admixture of sheer paganism. Some remote islands are still cannibal and there are heathen practices in many sections of this large area. Meanwhile some of the rarest instances of Christian power are found here. Whole islands have been completely changed into Christian communities. Several missionary agencies carry on the work and adventurous missionaries will be needed for a long time to complete the task. The Christian groups are increasingly independent and self-governing. They send their own missionaries to other islands or other sections of the peninsula. Missionary work is needed to counteract many adverse influences which issue from " civilization." Medical, educational and evangelistic work calls for further helpers.

12. PERSIA. A newly awakened country of much promise. The prevailing religion is the Shiah sect of Mohammedanism, very assertive and in many cases so fanatical that profession of the Christian faith swiftly led to martyrdom. Few lands have had more Christian martyrs, killed solely because of acceptance of Christ. There are many adherents of early forms of the Christian faith, most of the groups needing the reformation which did not reach them in the sixteenth century. Early missionaries tried to do all their work in connection with these groups and most of them still hope it

may be possible to unify and develop them. But it
has seemed necessary to organize the Moslem and
other converts into new churches for the present.
There are strong movements to bring about full
union of all these new groups at least, in hope that
the others may open their doors to them. For the
aid of those groups and for reaching the Moslems
who are now more amenable to Christian influences
than heretofore, missionaries will be needed for
some years.

13. THE PHILIPPINE ISLANDS. It was once considered that this was a Roman Catholic country,
but the opening of the land to other influences in
1898 revealed that it is far from being evangelized
in any sense. There are still savage tribes, pagan
and heathen in their practices, while there is the
same misreading of the Christian message which
is so widely found in Latin America under the influence of the Roman Catholic Church. From the
beginning of Protestant work earnest effort has
been made to avoid duplication of effort by a
widely adopted plan of comity. There is therefore
very little rivalry among the workers, though there
have been a surprising number of small groups of
believers formed, many of them having all the
marks of " sects." Several " unions " of these
groups have already occurred and the churches in
the Islands are for the most part quite independent
in creed and practice. Missionaries are still needed

and will serve largely in co-operation with native workers. Because of the educational work of the government there is less need for ordinary educational missionary work except for future Christian leadership. Medical work is less required for the same reason. But evangelistic missionaries have a wide and resultful field where they are warmly welcomed.

14. SIAM. One of the few small countries of the world which has always been independent and self-governing. It is the only country in which Buddhism is the state religion. The government is enlightened, but Buddhism is ingrained into most of its practices. The only opposition which Christianity experiences is social and historical. Parents send their children to Christian schools, but many of them refuse permission for them to be baptized when they wish to profess the Christian faith, and the missionaries do not baptize any minors without this consent. Missionary work has been conducted for about one hundred years, but was at first addressed largely to the Chinese residents. The first Siamese convert died only a short time ago and the present Siamese Christian group is of comparatively late origin. The major bodies of believers are still connected officially with Western churches, though their number is now large enough to constitute a national church. It is still an attractive field for missionary work.

15. SYRIA. If this term is allowed to include the little land of Palestine, it presents the most natural field for Christian service because of Christian history. The prevailing faith is Islam, together with a number of early and surviving Christian groups. For many years it was exceedingly dangerous for a Moslem convert to profess the Christian faith and for any Christian group to seek to present Christ to Moslems. This difficulty is reduced and the existing Christian bodies are making more effort to reveal Christ to their fellow-citizens. The land bids fair to become more important as highways develop into the Near East both for commerce and culture. Students come to the mission schools in Beirut from a very wide range; indeed, they come from the entire Arabic-speaking East. As approach to Moslems becomes less perilous the religious ministry of Syria will be more and more essential.

16. THIBET. This is the other closed country, into which no Christian believers are knowingly admitted. It is somewhat vague in outline but its population is about 3,500,000. The religion is a form of Buddhism and Hinduism combined in what is called Lamaism. Its adherents are zealous for the forms and rites of the faith, bitter against all innovations, scornful of all suggestions of improvement from the " infidel " outer world. Doubtless there is some knowledge of the Christian

faith among its people, both through the travels of nationals of that area and through the infiltration of Christian ideas from adjacent lands. Christian missionaries have settled as near to the borders as is permitted, both on the Chinese side and on the east, but none has been allowed to carry on any aggressive work in the land itself. When the time comes for entering Thibet the missionary cause will need men and women of the pioneer and martyr spirit. That time must soon come.

17. TURKEY. The reconstructive work in Turkey has been one of the outstanding results of the World War. Until that time it was a narrowly Moslem land, priding itself on its adherence to customs and procedures which were peculiar to itself. Under its present leadership the land has adopted many new customs, has opened the way for a multitude of new influences, and is rapidly gaining place among the more enlightened lands of the East. Christian work is carried on under severe restrictions still, but these restrictions will relax as the rulers themselves become more confident and less fearful of new movements. The change of long-standing Moslem practices has been naturally accompanied by some reactions among the more devoted Moslems and these believers tend to maintain the restrictions on all non-Moslem practices. Missionary work will soon be much more free and missionaries will find many enlight-

ened people in the Turkish area ready to consider the claims of Christ.

Such a detailed survey of the mission field is most unsatisfactory because conditions are constantly changing and words are no sooner written than they call for modification. The survey has the one value of indicating the continued need for thoughtful and well-directed missionary service. It reveals that the work is still needed if the purpose of Christ is to be carried out.

WHAT IS THE PRESENT CONDITION OF THE WORK?—A GENERAL SURVEY

IN this chapter an attempt is made to stand back from the work and view it as a whole, apart from geographical locations. Remember the earlier word, that in so wide a field everything is true and that nothing is so universally true that it might not need to be modified to match some conditions. Certain general conclusions may be thus summarized:

1. *The work is nowhere approaching completion in the major fields of missionary endeavour.* No one can estimate either the time or the forces necessary to complete the task in any given place. The movement may be speeded up by conditions which cannot be calculated. It may be delayed by similar forces. There is, in all lands, a vast amount of unorganized Christian sentiment. Christian ideas are undoubtedly permeating much of the thought of India, China, Japan and other lands.

A fairly typical illustration of this infusion of Christian ideas is the incident where a Moslem speaker at a meeting of the National Congress of India protested against Mr. Gandhi's policy of non-violent, passive resistance and against his entire leadership in Indian life. He exclaimed: "Where did Mr. Gandhi get this doctrine? Not from the Hindu Shastras and not from the Koran. He got it from Jesus Christ!" Mr. Gandhi would probably not deny the charge.

Church organizations are not so large as to warrant the amount of Christian influence which exists. There are many and powerful hindrances to the open and public confession of Christ. These hindrances might be suddenly or unexpectedly removed and in that case swift emergence of Christian life may occur. On the other hand, the hindrances may continue and be augmented, in which case Christian life may not develop increased force. Even with the growth of the present Christian force at the present rate of advance, one cannot pretend that the time is near when the aid of other Christian groups can be spared. This fact calls for anxious consideration of all methods of missionary work, to be sure that they are really helpful and are not a hindrance to the sound life of the new Christian groups in mission lands. Only ignorance of conditions in "missionary" lands can permit surprise that the work is not finished. There is much to hinder, much to overcome.

2. *The work is started everywhere but in Thibet and Afghanistan, where only incidental and indirect work has been attempted*. The most widespread enterprise of the human race is this of

making Christ known to all men. In some places
it is most ineffectively conducted, and this should
be corrected, but it is folly to measure the whole
enterprise by these instances. A careful report on
one mission land notes that " the results of the
work (in that land) are incredibly small when compared to the outlay of life and money." In another
land after eighty years of work there are only three
ordained national ministers of the Gospel and pain-
fully little spirit of aggression on the part of the
converts. Obviously, such frail beginnings after
years of work call for severe examination and
courageous correction of methods. Heroism does
not mean mere dogged continuance of work without results. As for the failures, most missionary
leaders can recognize without the names the instances which critics of the work use in their
adverse judgments. They are staple instances,
known and condemned by all leaders, but not typical of the whole work, whose beginnings and far
progress can be noted by any careful observer. It
would not be difficult to secure men and women
prepared for sacrifice even of life to begin work in
the two closed lands, but it is needless to make
sacrifices which cannot advance the work of the
Gospel.

3. *In all lands the missionary movement carries
the full programme of the Christian faith*. Theoretically the Christian movement might start
very simply, without institutions or organizations.

Practically it cannot go on without them, and their coming cannot be so simple as in the earliest Christian centuries, when they grew up quite unconsciously. In the present era these institutions have become a natural part of the Christian programme, emerging as soon as the movement gets under way. It was a long time before the first Christians established schools and hospitals and orphanages, a long time before they erected impressive buildings for worship and study. But all these things seem now such natural and inevitable parts of the Christian life that they appear among its first expressions. Hardly has the faith taken root in a land before the impulse toward schools and hospitals and other social agencies shows itself. In most lands nothing of the kind exists in the social order on a Christian scale or with the Christian spirit, and when these institutions are formed they become at once a burden on the Christian group. But the group is never strong enough to carry such a burden, and the sending countries must share it. Missionaries ordinarily inaugurate all these institutions, not at their own instance but at the desire of the new converts. The danger at once arises that the experience of the missionaries in their own lands will furnish their standard. The result is that in many lands the schools and colleges and hospitals, though natural accompaniments of the Christian faith, are scaled far above the financial and administrative ability of the Christian believers of the land. They must be carried in large part by funds and personnel from the sending countries.

It is easy to counsel that the institutions should be allowed to grow up spontaneously and only according to the ability of those whom they serve. With this theory most students of missions would agree. In practice it is exceedingly difficult. Is it not Christian duty to give the best one has or knows in the name of Christ? Can a physician follow in mission lands methods which have been outgrown and repudiated in his own land and not lay himself liable to condemnation? Can he have an insanitary hospital because the people of the land live in insanitary homes? Shall he omit an X-ray machine because it involves an expense which the national doctors could not provide? Shall he have an operating room that is protected against infections? It is true that in the earlier day his fathers did not have these things, but since he knows them and their bearing on successful handling of disease and wounds, can he avoid having them when he is acting in the name of Christ? Of course in emergencies any doctor will get along without them in America and elsewhere. But ought there to be a hospital bearing the Christian name which does not use the best methods normally available to the profession? The same questions apply to schools and to industrial enterprises.

The case is the more serious when young nationals of all these lands study in the West and see advanced and helpful methods in daily use. When they return to their own lands and find outworn and primitive methods used on their countrymen in the name of Christ, it does not commend the Gospel to them. Why are not their countrymen deserving of the best practices? A young doctor educated in Edinburgh or Baltimore, or a young teacher educated in New York or Chicago, or a young industrialist educated in Cornell or Michigan, knows the value of the latest methods in his line. He is doubtless ready to meet emergencies without them, but it is offensive to find institutions which bear the name of religion neglecting them or continuing in the use of antiquated and dangerous methods. It does not do to say that each person is entitled to the best conditions which he can support or that institutions ought to be only those which the locality can support. The whole procedure of the Christian movement is on other lines. There is always a large element of gift about it, as the Gospel itself is a gift and not a purchase.

There seems no escape from this problem except by the patience of time. In some cases the institutions are scaled higher than any necessity indicates; in these cases there has been error. But even in these cases our children may live to be grateful for the error, because standards have been set for the growing Christian group in the mission land. In all cases it is inevitable that missionaries who love Christ and the people whom they are serving will wish to do for the people the very best that can be done. Comparison with the first Christian century is quite beside the mark. These institutions are now inextricably interwoven with the programme of the Christian faith and wherever it starts they will emerge. If we could shut a mission land away from all other lands and let the Christian faith take again its original course, the early history might be repeated, but it is too late for that.

4. *In most lands the national church is developing in independence and self-reliance.* The progress is uneven and the world must not be judged by single instances, favourable or adverse. Missionary policies differ at this point. Some agencies lay large stress on the particular form which the Church must take. The Roman Catholic Church would hold that the Church can exist in only one form and with one organization. Other missionary bodies grade away from this extreme position toward the opposite one of complete abandonment of form or organization. It is the ideal of some bodies to form a world-wide organization of similar form, keeping the new groups closely related to the older and historical groups. Most agencies make no attempt to reproduce their own characteristic organizations. They aim to make Christ real to

new believers in assurance that He will form around Himself such organization as the place requires. This is better as a theory than it can ordinarily be in practice, because it is inevitable that a new organization will take its colour from the one with which the missionary leader is most familiar. Moreover, in every missionary group there are always some workers who count the history of their own Church part of the revelation of truth and are not willing to see its major details omitted in setting up a new body of believers. With the very best intentions of liberty, it is still probable that most guides take or send new travellers by the road they know best.

Still it is the wish of all missionary workers that the Church on the field shall be as independent as their own churches at home may be. They want what has been called for some years an " indigenous church," though they do not always agree on what such a church will be. The Jerusalem Council defined it in these terms:

A church, deeply rooted in God through Jesus Christ, an integral part of the Church Universal, may be said to be living and indigenous:

1. When its interpretation of Christ and its expression in worship and service, in customs and in art and architecture, incorporate the worthy characteristics of the people, while conserving at the same time the heritage of the Church in all lands and in all ages.

2. When through it the spirit of Jesus Christ in-

fluences all phases of life, bringing to His service all the potentialities of both men and women.

3. When it actively shares its life with the nation in which it finds itself.

4. When it is alert to the problems of the times and, as a spiritual force in the community, courageously and sympathetically makes its contribution to their solution.

5. When it is kindled with the missionary ardour and the pioneering spirit.

In such a church, the problem of discipline, polity, control, and financial support will naturally assume their proper places.

If this is a good description, it is also more or less ideal and few churches in mission lands have attained to it.

These churches do, however, in many instances begin to show their independence in the three lines that mark a church anywhere. (a) They have often written their own creeds, sometimes following the lines of the missionaries' creeds, sometimes diverging radically from them. This sometimes troubles the supporting churches. They forget that they themselves chose their own way of uttering their faith; they are so habituated to it that its original novelty is lost out of mind. The new churches must be allowed to make their own blunders or else they must be kept under control until they will accept the declarations of their founders.

(b) Many national churches have framed their own form of organization, their church polity. This is another difficulty for some sending churches, especially if they believe that their form of organization is the only one or even the best one among many. When this independence of organization is connected also with accepted Christian practices, such as the mode of baptism or the ordination of ministers, the case is more difficult still. For some sincere minds Christian history has settled these things and it seems a sheer waste of time and effort for another Church to blunder over the same path toward what must be the ultimate goal. Men hesitate to support a movement which does not carry with it the things they most believe in. So in all sending churches there are earnest people who refuse to support their own missionaries because they hear that the full truth and the full practice with which the Christian faith is associated in their experience is not maintained on the field.

(c) Many churches are also organizing their own expansion and their methods of practical work. Here there is least difficulty and on the whole the least independence. The financial element enters here most clearly. Aggressive work and existing organizations have to be sustained and the cost is often very large. Complete independence seems to mean loss of financial support when it seems most needed. The escape attempted in many places is in making funds available either to the new church alone or to some combination of mission and church. Experiments in this field are very many and very interesting. Nothing is yet cut-and-dried and no method is counted final. When the enterprise comes to the point where new personnel is not needed, it will be a problem how to inspire the Church with missionary zeal to send only money, and that money to be expended by people of whom it has no close knowledge and over whom it has no direction or control. At present the sending church can always call its own forces to account in their plans of work and their outlay of money. Manifestly it cannot do this so easily when the force is of another nationality, operating independently and on lines which the sending church cannot claim to understand. It will be a critical hour in the Christian movement when new missionaries are not needed, if missionary money is still needed. That hour has not yet come, but the problem begins to emerge on the present mission field. The gradualness of the emergence may be the saving of the Church, for it gives opportunity to adjust methods to it.

Criticism of the relation between missions and national churches is apt to be deserved somewhere but to be quite wide of the mark elsewhere. The relation is in all possible stages, and efforts to hasten the movement of independence are being made widely, sometimes with adverse results. A child can be made to walk too soon by over-ambitious parents, or he can be carried too long by over-tender parents. Each error is serious, but only sound sagacity and sincere love can take the middle and wise course.

5. *In all lands the divisions of Christendom have developed*. In only a few cases have these divisions occurred spontaneously on the field. Almost all have been carried to the mission lands by zealous adherents among missionary workers, though there are marked instances of separation inspired and led wholly by nationals. Some minds count this a wholesome and inevitable development; it indicates vitality and natural growth. They point out that religion, being so personal, very naturally encourages the independence of believers. Sects and parties are not a Christian phenomenon; they exist in all religions. Generally they constitute the ground of sharp discussion and antagonism. Indeed, in Western Christendom the relation between groups is on the whole kindlier now than in the East among religionists of other faiths. All talk of Christian groups being " at each other's throats " is sheer nonsense. They are prevailingly in close co-operation in actual work and attitudes.

It is still true, however, that most of the divisions of the West have certain historical backgrounds which are lacking in the newer lands of the East. This applies especially to the separations that have occurred in America. And it is also true that the divided groups in America do not generally desire believers in other lands to

follow similar courses. The trouble is that they
cannot always control their earnest workers on the
field, who cannot abide the errors which seem to
unsettle the essential faith. These workers encourage those whom they influence to withdraw
from their fellows in the interest of sound teaching
or wise practices. Most of these divided national
groups are the lengthened shadows of strong missionaries. They do not grow out of the soil and
are not an inherent development of natural Christian sentiment. Many movements for closer unity
on the field are thwarted by influences from the
West—by missionaries or their supporters who see
only evil in the proposed combinations.

6. It should be added at once that nowhere are
the churches of the West in closer co-operation
than on the mission field. The evils of division
are not escaped, but they are much less than in
the West. In many lands there are now National
Christian Councils unifying most of the forces.
In most lands the principle of comity rules, the
land or the population being assigned to the various agencies which are prepared to present Christ
there. In all lands there are agencies of co-
operation and united effort—colleges, hospitals,
industrial enterprises, in which many sending agencies join both in support and in direction. There
are union theological schools in mission lands which
the sending churches could not duplicate in their
own lands. Mission forces are much nearer the

ideal of making Christ central, without confusion
of forms or practices, than the forces in the sending
lands.

Indeed, the largest single co-operative Christian
body in the world is the International Missionary
Council, with headquarters in London and New
York. It includes in its membership more church
bodies than any other one organization in the
world. In the United States the same distinction
is held by the North American Conference of Foreign Missions. No other agency is able to correlate
so many Church Boards and Committees and to
bring them into conference. It has no legislative
or administrative functions, but it insures an understanding among all these missionary agencies,
and it has served an excellent purpose of reference
and counsel among them. Through these co-
operative bodies certain lines of service are carried on which each Board could do less effectively
by itself.

Criticism of collision between missionary agencies, of needless separations among new believers,
of the extension to these lands of controversies born
of Western conditions, can unhappily be sustained
by too many instances. The criticism is often deserved and should be taken to heart by many of
these agencies. In all frankness it must be said
that many of these instances arise from the presence and work of missionary agencies independent
of any one church and supported by distinctive

groups who are out of sympathy with the churches of which they are a part. In such cases it is clear that the churches themselves cannot be responsible. Long after these churches in the West are amicable on a disputed matter, individual members may be sorely troubled and belligerent about it. If their Mission Boards do not continue the controversy, there is nothing to hinder their founding another organization which will carry the issue over seas. Criticism of missionary work ought to take this factor into account. The independent societies are entirely within their rights in undertaking missionary work, and it is natural that the issues which brought them into being will seem vital and essential to the workers whom they send abroad. In many lands efforts are made to draw believers of certain types among missionaries and nationals into offensive or defensive groups. The leaders in these groups are seldom nationals; they are missionaries who represent similar groups in the West. These divided or divisive groups are apt to be quite small there as here, but rather assertive.

The prevailing spirit of the Christian group is toward unity, and this appears nowhere more decidedly than on the mission field. Indeed, some cases of union are embarrassing and questionable in their breadth and inclusiveness. For, after all, the Christian faith is not just anything anybody happens to be thinking at a given moment. Christians cannot unite with everybody, but fraternity should be denied only when the other groups are also denied Christian standing.   When fellowship is refused, the implication must always be that the excluded person or group is less than or other than Christian.   This is a solemn implication which ought to make all believers pause.

VIII

WHAT ARE THE CRITICAL NEEDS OF THE ENTERPRISE AT THIS JUNCTURE?

WITH all its encouragements, there are some conditions in the missionary enterprise which give its supporters concern and raise grave questions among responsible administrators and field workers. They give no ground for doubt of its victory or outcome, but they do preclude placid acceptance of its *status quo*. This is especially important just now when approach to all parts of the world is so feasible. During his stay in India as the Joseph Cook lecturer in 1931-32, someone quoted to Dr. J. Harry Cotton the saying that " the gates are not merely ajar; the hinges are removed." With a few exceptions this is a world condition.

Yet the enterprise is not moving forward as might be hoped and has been expected. Whether the hindrance lies on the field or in the home Church, in the working force or the administrative force, or the supporting force, may be discussed. The Jerusalem Council closed with a prayer paper which the Bishop of Salisbury counted an expression of the deepest needs of the missionary movement. He says they were "worked out by the promoters of the Council through agonies of helplessness; we were driven to them by the experience of our own sore need." These "deepest needs" were eight in number: a missionary spirit, a spirit of prayer, a spirit of sacrifice, a spirit of unity, a spirit of witness, a spirit of self-offering, a spirit of interpretation, and the completion of our conversion. Obviously no final word can be said on such a subject because the conditions change from time to time. Some critical needs seem to emerge just now, however, some new and some perennial.

1. *There is need for a clearer understanding and fuller acceptance of the main objective of missions.* The widening of methods and of programmes has resulted in confusion at this critical point. Methods easily become ends in themselves or they may be so conducted as to thwart the main purpose of the enterprise. Every vital movement needs to keep its major objective in clear sight because of this tendency. Educators in the West are facing this just now. Huge endowments, immense buildings, multiplied courses of instruction, accent on specialties, development of departments—all these things may be made important in themselves and so obscure the reason for their own existence. Thoughtful men are asking how to control the means for the sake of the real end, and for that reason are asking just what the main objective of education is.

In the field of missions, because of the variety of churches, and workers concerned, complete agreement has never existed. And it is certain that the objective of so great an enterprise in so wide an area and with so vast an appeal to world population cannot be stated narrowly nor dogmatically with any hope of acceptance.

(a) The objective must be something valuable enough to be worth doing at the large cost of life and gift that is required. This is a safeguard against extremes everywhere. Some proposals for missionary work are frankly not worth while, and no great enthusiasm can be aroused for them. They may attempt so little that no one would sacrifice for the result, or they may attempt something so temporary that it is not worth the necessary time and trouble. The test of any proposed objective will be, in part, whether it will inspire men and women to sacrifice life and money in its behalf. Will it send men away from home across the world *and keep them there?* It is not enough to find something that will last during a spurt of zeal; the real thing must explain hundreds of men staying on the ground when so much is against them that other men leave the field. Anybody can go, for almost any reason. It is not so easy to find reasons for sticking it out year in and year out. And will the objective inspire men to give sacrificially and to keep on doing it year after year after the first burst of interest has subsided? Sob-stories can start the flow of gifts, but deeper springs must be tapped if the flow is to continue.

(*b*) The objective must be great enough to justify the disturbance of human life, which it always causes, at the receiving end. It is no light thing to enter a social situation and upheave it as the Christian faith does. No slight purpose can justify the replacing of one religious faith by another; yet this is implied in the missionary enterprise. Those who are accustomed to the social and personal requirements of the Christian faith can hardly realize what they mean to people in an entirely different social setting. Many observers oppose or question the missionary enterprise at just this point. Unless something very serious is intended or needed, missionary work seems a sheer impertinence and interference. These lines are being written on the campus of a great American university and it is perfectly certain that if one went out on the campus and asked the average instructor or student his attitude toward foreign missions, the opposition expressed would be mainly on this line. Cloudy vision of the main objective is part of the reason for lax support of the work throughout the Church in America.

(*c*) The objective must be great enough to include the wide variety of methods or approaches which the work has developed. Most of these methods have emerged without any definite purpose or planning. They have been merely the

naturally next thing to be done. Few early workers went out to found orphanages or to care for
lepers or to plant primary schools. An occasional
worker like Alexander Duff saw in education a sure
way of overthrowing religious superstition and
giving Christian truth its chance, but until the
educational method had become quite fully established, missionary agencies did not send out workers distinctively trained for it. The history of
medical missions runs in the same lines. Originally
medical workers were sent to care for missionaries,
not for nationals. They were expected to be evangelists except when missionaries needed medical
attention. Medical missions really grew out of
the major purpose of missions. Actual work for
the sick and distressed as a method in itself was a
later thought. So do the new rural programme
and the industrial plans. The main objective cannot shut out such methods without reckoning with
the normal history of Christian progress. The root
must somehow be adequate for the natural fruit.
This means that the necessary purposes shall find
shelter in the main objective, shall serve it and yet
remain worthy in themselves.

The most marked current discussions in intimate
missionary circles bear on this issue. It was the
central theme of the 1932 meeting of The International Missionary Council at Herrnhut. The
Scandinavian and Northern European missionaries
felt that in the West the social services of the

Gospel have been over-accented, that too much dependence has been placed upon external methods of helping the souls of men and not enough on fundamentally spiritual methods. They urge workers to recognize frankly that there are some things which only the Spirit of God can do and that too much temporal machinery tends to minimize the power and place of the Spirit. They call Americans " activists." The missionary leaders in the West in turn urge that there are great hindrances to the hearing and accepting of the message of Christ which need to be cleared in order to give that Gospel its full opportunity; moreover, that the Gospel finds part of its missionary argument in its power to set the whole life of man free from its hampering conditions. They acknowledge that in many cases this secondary service has been so magnified as to obscure the primary service, but they do not admit that it is any less part of the missionary enterprise.

At Herrnhut steps were taken toward clearer agreement. They involved a full acceptance of the central spiritual purpose of the whole work, that the major appeal is not to men as belonging to this world alone but to their eternal value. At the same time it was agreed that these beings of eternal value do live their lives here and now under conditions which make or mar their development toward the personalities which are God's gracious will for them. All methods must serve this inner and essential value of humanity, even though they may seem to end with the present life. Men are not to become eternal when they die; they are eternal in this life. Their immortality and spiritual value will not be created by the fact of death; it will be merely revealed in that fact. The Jerusalem Council said:

The end of Christian missions is nothing less than the production of Christlike character in individuals and societies and nations through faith in and fellowship with Christ the living Saviour, and through corporate sharing of life in a divine society.

Some of our work loses sight of the necessity for " faith in " Christ the living Saviour. Or it seeks to produce the Christlike character in other ways, by social changes and improved conditions, whereas the order must be maintained—there needs to be an increased number of changed men, men of " faith in and fellowship with Christ the living Saviour," so that the wider and fuller programme may be carried forward to success.

Many things have occurred in Western life to cloud this issue. There is no hope of carrying on unitedly and strongly unless we can see more clearly what we are trying to do. We must at least see how our varied service fits into some scheme large enough to take it all in, or we shall work at cross purposes. We need a reassertion of spiritual values, of the unique and essential place of Christ in the hope of men, of the applicability of the spirit and principles of Christ to the whole of life and to every life. A thoughtful traveller, fresh from world experience, wrote on this point:

I am quite ready to urge extreme cordiality, sympathy and friendliness on the part of missionaries toward representatives of other religions; and the complete abandonment of the attitude of antagonism. But I am not ready to stand for any merging of religions, or any abandonment of our sense of the unique or surpassing significance of Jesus Christ and His religion for every man, woman and child on the face of the earth. Neither am I ready to give up Paul's finely expressed hope, that a day will come when " at the name of Jesus every knee will bow, and every tongue confess that He is Lord . . ." I like something a friend said to me in Tokyo: " I am quite willing a Buddhist should take Buddha for his Moses; but I am not willing he should take Buddha for his Christ."

If we are not giving to our fellows an essential gift, a gift above anything which they now have, we will not allow our duty to cut deeply into our convenience or comfort. We must decide that what we are doing really matters in the present and eternal life of humanity. The issue is far deeper than a question of missions; it is a question of religion itself and within the sphere of religion a question of the permanent and essential value of the Christian faith. This involves an estimate of the person and work of Christ. For the sake of our world obligation we need a revival of clear thinking at all these points. At the close of the Parliament of Religions in 1893, a Hindu Brahmin remarked: " The world may just as well note that the religion of the Babe of Bethlehem, which in three short centuries made its way to the throne of Imperial Rome and since then has pervaded the Western world, is slowly but surely becoming the universal religion." He then called upon the Parliament to offer the Lord's Prayer because it expressed the fundamental religion which all could recognize. That was forty years ago. Would he make the same prophecy about Christianity now? Is this what Christian believers now assert?

2. There is needed at this time *an increase of missionary force at important points and in important elements.* The force may well become less static, more mobile, less fixed at centres and more capable of moving to emergency locations. It must be of the highest quality also, prepared to meet even more demanding requirements than heretofore. There has come to be a feeling that the work of the missionary is ended, either because of changed religious sentiment or because of the development of the national churches. Neither reason is justified. There are a few places where the existing force may be gradually diminished. But these are not typical points. At some places there needs to be a good body of evangelistic recruits. Thibet and Afghanistan are not yet occupied at all,

as we have noted. Great areas of Africa, China, Latin America and Asia have not been entered effectively by the Christian forces and it is too much to expect that the present small national churches will be able to enter them except after long delay.

Moreover, the Christian programme has been greatly increased and additional workers will be needed for new phases. We are just entering on rural service—not to teach the elements of agriculture for its own sake, helpful as that would be, but to serve all the needs of men who live in the difficult rural areas of the world. The need for imported teachers is not apt to increase in much of the world, though education is still too heavy a task for many nations. More medical missionaries are needed, distributed over sections of the earth where medical development has been retarded. Industrial workers have a large service yet to render in the name of Christ, especially in the Orient where modern industrialism constitutes so large a social problem.

Many missionary leaders call for a number of demonstration centres, manned by capable workers who will study local needs and find ways of approach which can be applied to wide areas. For many national churches it would be helpful if a specimen instance of effective and feasible evangelistic work could be developed. Similar demonstrations could be made in all forms of social service. It is the application of the "project method" in attempting typical areas. The programme should not be scaled beyond the possibilities of the people, but it should use the best and most resultful methods. It should save the younger churches from needless experimentation at such points, demonstrating how the Gospel can be extended and applied among their own people in their own lands.

All this means that there remains real missionary work to be done. Most of it is still of the pioneer order, independent of physical convenience and comfort. At many points there is need for more "frugal, pioneering courage." Life on the mission field, as everywhere else, easily gets soft and agreeable at cost to its real efficiency. The days of great missionary labour are not over; there are lines of service and places of living which provide for all that the most heroic days offered.

3. There is critical need just now for *the development of a national leadership, especially a lay leadership, independent of all foreign support or reliance*. As the Church on the field grows, it becomes more apparent that it must acquire a character suited to its own land. It may use much that comes from other lands, but it should do this by its own will and not from any necessity. The weakest point of most national churches is in their lay force, the men and women who draw no financial support from the mission or Church and do

not depend for their livelihood on their religious
work. Most of the training in leadership on the
mission field faces toward the ministry or some
form of definite and whole-time Christian service.
The need for this cannot be debated, but it is
always dangerous when a Church rests exclusively
on those who live by its ministry. The strength
of a true Christian Church is in its laity, the men
and women who live day by day in demonstration
of the spirit of Christ. The professional or supported element in the Church tends to draw the
work away from its natural lines, copying what
they see in others or what they have learned from
books.

Along with this lay leadership there must continue to be developed the technical leadership
which is already so strong in some lands. It now
becomes a serious question how far missionaries
should be responsible for the maintenance and direction of the institutions in which these leaders
get their training. So long as the training is in
foreign hands it will inevitably partake in some
degree of foreign spirit and methods. This may
be excellent or it may be very bad. At the same
time, it is no simple matter to turn over to new and
inexperienced believers the work of the future
church, thus breaking the young church away from
the older churches before it has had a chance to
absorb the real life of its new faith. In most lands
this work passes into national hands as rapidly as

experienced workers emerge. The process cannot be hastened unduly without peril to the nascent Church. Along with this one must note with concern that some well-equipped nationals are un-willing to make the sacrifices which are expected of missionaries; larger salaries have sometimes to be paid to these nationals than are paid to mis-sionaries in similar positions, not merely because of the many dependents who fall upon them when they find places of influence, but because they have been trained in the West and are accustomed to ways of living which the missionaries forego and they are not prepared to forego. Missionary lead-ers and Christian believers in all lands need to keep a clear sight of what have been called " the veracities " involved in their estimate of " inde-pendent " churches, not calling them so when they are not so, nor pretending that they are carrying their own burden when they are not doing so. And the long delay in bringing such churches into being calls for careful and unsparing examination of missionary and church methods now in use.

4. There is need for *the correction of the dis-unions which mar the work both in the supporting force at home and its operating force on the field*. The preceding chapter has warned against exag-geration here. Critics or enemies of the work always over-accent the differences among Christian believers. There is large co-operation already; union movements are vigorous and promising in

many fields; differences among believers are not
allowed to hinder close fellowship. Nor is it at
all suggested that complete uniformity is desirable,
even if it were feasible. The fact is that the greatest work of missions in the past has actually been
done by a divided Church. This does not dispar-
age the work of the Roman Catholic Church with
its binding unity. Yet it is true that the Protestant
work, done by a divided Church, bears very favourable comparison with anything accomplished
by this undivided Church. Some of us would
hesitate long before trying to bring the entire
Protestant Church into organic and institutional
uniformity. No such programme is needed for
the desired result.

But no one can observe without a deep pain in
his heart the multitude of groups formed in mission lands around ideas which mean little or
nothing, to most of them, ideas which they have
been taught by visitors who have been reared in
them. These new believers have not had their fair
chance to follow Christ as they have seen Him.
Sometimes a hand has been reached across the sea
and large-hearted workers have been told that they
must not follow the impulses of their hearts but
must adhere to practices and beliefs which mark
their supporters at home. Sometimes no such hand
has been needed, but speakers and papers have
brought from the field the sad story of " the defec-
tion of fellow-workers " and warnings from their

colleagues that they are not to be trusted. The ungodly are treated to the spectacle of brethren disputing one against another, using time and strength which might well be spent in other service.

Although organic unity and uniformity are not necessary, yet many unions ought to occur in every Christian land. Many of the divisions both mar our witness and disgrace us, both by their spirit and their outcome. The word of Professor Mac-Murray, then of Balliol College, Oxford, is not too strong—" The disunity of the churches is a confessed scandal." No wonder he then asks, " Why, then, does it continue? " But there are separations which are wise and helpful, not implying division of spirit. There are differences of administration as there are differences of temperament. But there can be an underlying fellowship which will prevent thoughtful men from counting ours a divided and discordant witness. If we can trust the same Master we can believe in each other.

Instead, mark the pathos of the discussion which occurred in London near the end of 1931, which came to the present writer in an Indian newspaper: Cardinal Bourne, of the Roman Catholic Church, had noted a mass to be said in the Slavonic rite in his cathedral, in which, because no word would be intelligible to any present, it would be proper for every Catholic to participate. He then added: " But to the Anglican who would ask us to join in morning prayer or evening prayer, every word of which we can understand, we

have but one answer to make—that of the blessed
martyr, Margaret Clitherow: ' I will not pray with you
nor shall you pray with me, neither shall I say Amen to
your prayer nor shall you say it to mine! ' "   The only
condition on which Roman priests are allowed to be
present at a great demonstration for world peace was
that no vocal prayer should be uttered.   This is one of
the incredible survivals of an era which we all hoped
had gone.   But alas, it is not so certain that we Protestants have entirely escaped that bad era.

There are some things we cannot yet do together,
though they are distinctive Christian things.   That
is, we have set limits on our Christian association,
not in minor or unimportant matters but in deeply
vital actions.   Our faith has made us vigorous in
its defence but we have not learned how to distinguish between enemies and friends.

This confusion runs out to the field at many
points and weakens our witness to a non-Christian
world.   Unless we can gather our differences under
some large agreements and manifest to all the
world that we differ amid these central agreements
we shall have to go on with a limited and weak-
ened ministry to men whom Christ seeks to win
to Himself.   How can we tell distracted and divided China that its hope is in the unifying Christ,
when China has good reason to know that we who
know Christ will not allow Him to unite us, but
instead make Him a reason for dividing asunder?

5. *There is critical need for a more adequate
literature for the growing national churches, in-*

volving increased appeal to the intellectual groups.
The Christian movement often starts with the
lower levels of society and reaches the higher levels
later. An occasional Paul in any land, but the rank
and file are simpler. Meanwhile, the believers on
the lower levels are soon lifted, their children
having advantages beyond many on the higher
levels. The need for foreign literature therefore
emerges very early. The Christian mind has to
be fed or it weakens and becomes erratic. The
Bible is a great asset of the Christian faith because it is almost immediately made available for
believers and they are encouraged or required to
use it. But the Bible is a book-making book, and
it is seldom left alone. It starts the current of
literature everywhere when that current is not
already running. The result is that even among
illiterate populations there soon develops a read-
ing constituency whose need must be supplied.

This is a weak place in present mission development. Earnest effort is made to strengthen it by
the organization of effective Christian Literature
Societies in most mission lands. Two types of
Christian literature are provided: translations of
existing literature and original productions by national believers. Translations are naturally first
but often the most effective productions are those
of gifted nationals. One Japanese Christian writer
has produced two or three religious books which
have become " best sellers " throughout the land.

Many of the most widely read books in China and India are productions of nationals.

The matter for concern is the small quantity of such material for groups who cannot be appealed to except by thoughtful writing which is in creditable form and language. The lack is partly made up by the increased familiarity of such groups with the English language. But nothing will take the place of books and other literature available in the familiar tongue.

Increased appeal should be made to the intellectual groups. This does not imply that they are more important in the sight and love of God than the plainest people. It does imply that they have their own value in God's sight and deserve as much consideration on their own terms and their own level as simpler folk. They are not to be neglected any more than others. But the appeal has to be made to them in terms suited to their needs. In several mission lands definite efforts are made to meet and cultivate them. The Round Table Conferences in India, the Conferences in Latin America, the university gatherings in China, student gatherings in Persia and many other lands,—all these are contributions to the supply of this serious need. It is true that God has not chosen many wise and mighty (I Cor. 1:26), but He has chosen some in every emergency and every period of His Church. An observer once said that the most spiritually neglected group in New York City were the rich; much more was done for the poor than for them, yet their souls were as precious in the sight of God. This is true of the average mission land regarding the intellectuals. They will be reached partly by direct personal effort and partly by a Christian literature which moves on their level. Missions and Boards are beginning to take this need seriously, but much more needs to be done before the situation is cleared.

6. *There is critical need for an increased consideration of the whole work in the home Church.* There is some direct opposition to the missionary enterprise in the Church in America, but there is very much more preoccupation and consequent neglect of its claims.

(*a*) Part of the opposition arises from relaxed conviction of the validity and necessity of the work of Christ anywhere. If He has no essential place in America, He would manifestly have none elsewhere. If He is merely desirable in life, there will be no sacrificial effort to make Him known to other lands. Desirable things can be replaced by less desirable things; essential things cannot be replaced. Permanent supporters of missionary work are prevailingly those who consider Christ essential. If their number decreases, the support of the work decreases. The increase of their number is one necessity for the future of the enterprise.

(*b*) Part of the indifference of home-staying Christians arises from the increased volume of

news from mission lands, some of it adverse to
missionary results and some of it over-laudatory or
over-condemnatory of those lands. By one opinion
they do not need mission work; by another opinion
they could not appreciate the gift of Christ nor
welcome the missionaries. Informed and intelligent missionary advocates learn nothing new from
this increased volume of information. It has been
known from the first. But to the half-informed
and lightly convinced it comes with surprise and
unsettlement. A whole new campaign of information is needed—not the standard Mission Study
programme of books and courses, valuable as it is
and important to maintain—but more general information, addressed to people who will not attend
schools of missions and who must be reached from
informed pulpits and through attractive and au-
thoritative publications. It is a bad sign of the
times that religious periodicals have so largely lost
their power in church life. Nothing has taken their
place as channels of information on matters vital
to the progress of the faith. Meanwhile, large use
ought to be made under intelligent direction of the
secular press, whose authorities prevailingly are
ready to co-operate in spreading this news.

(c) Part of the neglect of missions abroad is due
to the increased pressure of needs and plans in
the home lands. Building programmes for local
churches would seem to our fathers incredibly extensive and expensive. They often overburden a

congregation until any appeal for work outside the parish seems cruel. When, on the heels of these enormous plans, there comes an economic disturbance, the situation grows doubly difficult. The responsibility of the Christian Church for human life has greatly widened in recent years and many a church carries a load which earlier churches never undertook. This makes consideration of world needs all the more complicating.

Pressure of home needs has also resulted in the practice of "lumping" the whole appeal for benevolences in one universal budget and subscription. The effect of this plan is to swallow up the distinctive call of the world situation in a general call for help outside the parish. Nowhere has this plan increased foreign mission support; in many instances it has markedly decreased it. Theoretically it is "all one work," as many say. Practically the world phases of the enterprise have qualities which do not lie in the other phases. Separating them and giving them sharp emphasis does not lessen the appeal of other parts of the total work; instead, it aids these other parts. But the world enterprise needs to be reinstated in the Church mind as a distinctive work which can be carried on only under high motives and with intelligent understanding.

If the nerve of missions has been cut anywhere, it is here in the heart of the home Church. It is here also that it must be restored and renewed.

Hard times do not affect the command of Christ. This command was not postulated on prosperity. Slackening such work because it requires sacrifice and self-denial would be utterly illogical in adherents of a religion born at a cross. The Christian symbol embodies the idea of doing hard things without hesitation. Balking before them would belie the faith.

Mission Boards, administrative agencies, missionaries themselves are only incidental to the main task. The real burden lies on Christian believers, led chiefly by pastors and church officials. It is they who will bring the revival of concern and interest. They may be aided from the mission field, but only aided.

In the winter of 1932-33 the British Isles are to witness two experiments in this service. The Anglican Church has commandeered the services of Bishop Linton, missionary in Persia, to conduct a church-wide campaign for the renewal of spiritual life. It is not primarily missionary, but all informed people know that when the spiritual life is revived it will express itself in missionary outreach. The major hope is that the home Church will be stirred within its own borders; its indifference is a burden on the hearts of all earnest believers.

The other experiment is the coming from India of a group of National Christians, not to plead for missions nor to increase gifts for India, but to share with the people of the old country the fer-

vour and fresh joy of their fresh experience with
Christ. The Jerusalem Council expressed the hope
that ere long the younger church of missionary
lands might send ambassadors of spiritual power
to the older churches of the West. In small ways
this has already been done, in the coming of individual outstanding Christian leaders from most of
the mission lands. In this case there will be a
group, carefully selected, to bring inspiration to
their Christian brethren, making some slight return
for the gift sent them through the century.

Both these experiments will be observed with
care and with large hopefulness. With an awakened Church, sensing anew the value and necessity
of Christ in its own life, there will be no question
of a cut or injured missionary nerve. That nerve
will prove itself alive and tingling and will direct
the Church into efficient support of this, its central
work.

A BRIEF BIBLIOGRAPHY

THE current literature of missions is very extensive.
Each chapter of this book could be heavily documented.
Yet the movement is in such rapid progress that most
books and magazines soon pass out of use; they are out
of date as soon as they are issued. There are, however,
publications which have permanent value for the present generation. A few of these may be noted here.

The two necessary magazines are: *The International
Review of Missions,* published quarterly in London and

New York, the organ of the International Missionary Council, 419 Fourth Avenue, New York, ($2.50 a year); and *The Missionary Review of the World,* published monthly at 156 Fifth Avenue, New York ($2.50 a year). The former deals with the larger problems and the philosophy of missions, the latter with its current progress. Each is of high value to thoughtful students of this world movement.

Most mission Boards issue full annual reports and also current publications which are available free or at small expense to applicants. They generally contain ample answers to local criticisms or objections regarding the enterprise. Churchmen might well secure these reports and publications as issued by their own Boards.

All missionary publications of recent years make frequent reference, as this book does, to the Jerusalem Meeting of the International Missionary Council. The Report of this meeting is issued in eight small volumes which are almost essential to libraries and thoughtful observers of the movement as it actually is. Their material will be of value throughout the generation now living. They can be secured from the International Missionary Council, 419 Fourth Avenue, New York, or through the publishers of this book.

The following books will carry the studies farther on their special lines:

Robert E. Speer, *The Unfinished Task of Foreign Missions,* (1926);

Stephen J. Corey, *The Minister and His Missionary Message,* (1931);

Cleland B. McAfee, *Changing Foreign Missions,* (1926);

John R. Mott, *The Present-Day Summons to the World Mission of Christianity,* (1932);

Cornelius H. Patton, *God's World,* (1932);

William Paton, *A Faith for the World*, (1929);

Arthur J. Brown, *The Foreign Missionary*, (13th Edition, 1932);

Basil Matthews, *The Clash of World Forces*, (1931);

William Owen Carver, *The Course of Christian Missions*, (1932);

Stacy R. Warburton, *The Making of Modern Missions*, (1931).

Any of these books can be secured from the publishers of this volume, or from other book-dealers, and will be found in many public libraries.

Printed in the United States of America